The Last American Cowboy

Resilience During Life's Entanglements: Surviving the Invisible Darkness of Bipolar Disorder

by Moses Jade

Copyright

The Last American Cowboy

Resilience During Life's Entanglements: Surviving The Invisible Darkness of Bipolar Disorder

ISBN: 978-1-7359479-2-1 (Paperback)
ISBN: 978-1-7359479-3-8 (eBook)

Library of Congress Control Number: 9781735947921

The author and publisher have made every effort to ensure the information in this book was accurate and complete at press time. We have tried to recreate events and conversations from the past, and memories from those moments in time. The author and publisher do not assume, and hereby disclaim any liability to any party for any loss, damage or disruption cause by errors or omissions, whether such errors or omissions result from negligence, accident, or any other cause.

Publisher: Top Tea Food Fuel International (A Non-Profit Corporation)
10555 Turtlewood Court #1905
Houston TX 77072

First Edition November 2020

Table of Contents

La Pantera productions

FINANCING
DADS
EXSPOSURE
BOMB
TEST
PAYBACK

This will make sense after reading the first Chapter (aka, "Episodes")

Introduction

Chris Kelly is an interesting man and his story is worth telling. He is a complex mixture of honesty and integrity, with a passion for helping others. Chris doesn't waste words when he communicates. Some feel he's blunt, but, there are deep thoughts behind those intensely focused unblinking eyes.

Many famous people either have or had Bipolar Disorder: Mel Gibson, Carrie Fisher, Jimi Hendrix, Kurt Cobain and Winston Churchill to name a few.[1] Chris didn't quite live the same life as these famous people, but he had similar struggles.

People with Bipolar Disorder experience extreme highs and lows. On the low side, feelings of depression, anxiety and a desire to isolate themselves for long periods of time. On the high side, extreme optimism, making people laugh, talking to everyone they see with an unbridled energy.

Maybe some reading his story will feel sad, others may feel happy, but what if those feelings were experienced so intensely on either end of the emotional spectrum that you could not function? This was Chris' life before he learned to manage his condition because he suffers from Bipolar Disorder.

Interviewing Chris to write this book was a thrill. Seeing his eyes light up when he would recall a story, which led to another story; then another. Using the internet for research helped corroborate Chris' stories with facts, times, places and sometimes dates.

The main goal of collecting Chris' life experiences and telling the world his story is threefold:
1. Help others learn life's lessons
2. Experience the world through the eyes of 2.8% of the world's population
3. Understand that no matter how bad your situation, you can find a way out

What do we mean by 2.8%? Depending on which study you believe, it is estimated that between one and three percent of adults in the U.S. suffer from Bipolar Disorder. While the disorder usually begins in adolescence or early adulthood, it can sometimes start as late as 40 or 50 years old.[2]

Only half of the people in the world with bipolar disorder understand their condition and seek treatment. Unfortunately, almost 20% of those untreated will commit suicide, but their deaths are just ruled as a suicide and lumped in with the 1% of the population that take their own lives. As many as 50% of those with bipolar disorder attempt suicide every year.[3]

About the Book

The goal of this book is for the reader to get a glimpse into the life of someone with Bipolar Disorder, somewhat structured in the way someone with bipolar may think, which is unstructured and non-sequential. Therefore, the book is organized by chapters which are more like headlines (called "Episodes") as a method to group stories based on major events in Chris Kelly's life.

The reader will have a comprehensive understanding of Chris only after consuming the entire book. He was in many situations and learned many life lessons along the way, which are shared through his stories. Since the times spent interviewing Chris created a meandering path, only after his stories were gathered was the decision made to sequence the book accordingly.

F I X T H E

GLITCH

copyright 2012 two u

Chris expresses himself by creating his "logos", and using today's vernacular, many people will call them memes.

People that are Bipolar need to focus more intently than those without the disorder because their thoughts are all over the place. Oftentimes conversations are confusing because people with this condition talk a lot and switch topics often, sometimes making it difficult for others to follow. In their minds all topics are connected to all other topics, so why don't other people understand that? Chris describes it best in this text he sent while writing the book:

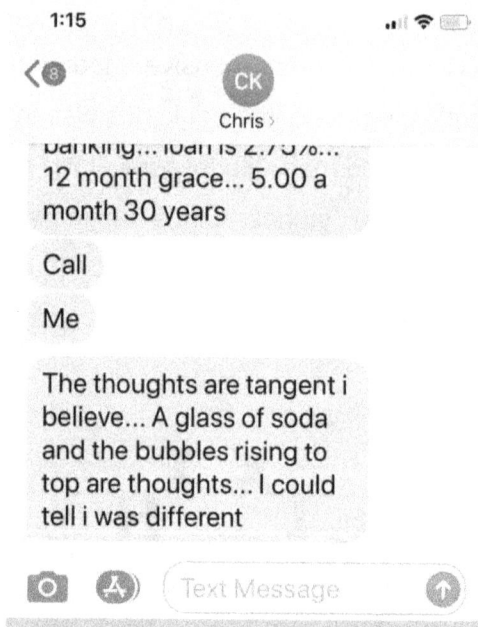

1:15

CK

Chris ›

banking... loan is 2.75%...
12 month grace... 5.00 a
month 30 years

Call

Me

The thoughts are tangent i
believe... A glass of soda
and the bubbles rising to
top are thoughts... I could
tell i was different

Text Message

Chris believes he was born with Bipolar Disorder, but it didn't manifest itself in his day-to-day life until after a series of emotionally jarring events. Our hope in sharing Chris' story with the world is to help others realize that many people with mental disorders can learn to cope. But the first step to coping is learning something is wrong and then taking appropriate, incremental actions to improve, like Chris.

Both biographies and autobiographies encompass the story of someone's life and are usually written in a chronological fashion, this is neither, and both at the same time. Biographies are written by someone else in the third person and autobiographies are written by the subject in the first person. This book is an interesting hybrid. A few emails and texts, but mostly interviews were used to record stories and situations that influenced Chris' life and have made him who he is today.

Along with raising awareness of Bipolar Disorder by publishing this book, we are helping to fund research to help those struggling with a mental illness:

Up to 10% of profits from this book will be donated annually to:

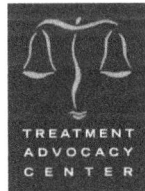

Treatment Advocacy Center
"Eliminating Barriers to the Treatment of Mental Illness".

Chris Has a Dream: To Help Those in Need

The Foster Care system in the United States is broken and there are no plans or regulations to fix it in the future. "Our youth are our future" according to Chris, so we need to make investments that will help young people thrive. He hopes to create a model that other states will adopt with the Greater Houston chapter being the first of its kind in the country.

With appropriate oversight, Chris' dream is to build a facility to provide a foster care environment with structured learning experiences, activities, counseling and community involvement of internship, mentoring, college and trade skill preparation. Here are some shocking statistics uncovered while writing this book, children in Foster Care are:

- Four times more likely to be abused than children of their same age
- Twenty-eight (28) times more likely to be abused when living in a group home
- One-third reported abuse by their Foster Parent

States have admitted that no assurances are in place to care for these children. What's worse? More than 50% of the children recovered by the FBI after busting human trafficking rings came from foster homes.[4]

What's worse? Children will "age out" of the system between the ages of 18 and 21. Within four years 50% of those children have no income; the other 50% are earning on average less than $7,500 annually. Despite the country averaging 34 million entry-level jobs open each year, these 30,000 Foster Care dependents are unable to support themselves. Many will become homeless or worse.[5]

Episode 1: Who Was "Big Mike"?

Most biographies and autobiographies start with basic information about the subject, name, birthplace, upbringing, and life story. This book is different, so we're going to start it differently. This book starts with Chris' father, before Chris was born.

Chris had long suspected he was different than everyone else in some way, but he didn't receive a professional diagnosis until in his 40's and only after a series of triggering events. As he reflects on where he is today and after receiving the official diagnosis from his counselor that he is "bipolar", Chris often wonders how his father's assignment in the Marshall Islands may have affected his mental development. Before learning specifically about Francis' assignment, it's probably helpful to bring you up to speed on the US and its interests in the Marshall Islands after World War II.

Bikini Atoll, Marshall Islands

In 1944, The United States took over the Marshall Islands from Japan and decided to make it the proving grounds for nuclear weapon testing. The Marshall Islands are a beautiful expanse of white sandy beaches and coral reefs. Islanders living in Bikini Atoll were evacuated and the island was readied for testing. Formerly known as Eschscholtz Atoll in the 1800s, the area consisted of 23 islands made up of almost 230 square miles of lagoon. The US conducted 23 nuclear tests from 1946-1958. Tests took place on the reef, in the air and underwater.

Chris' father enlisted in the US Air Force on December 19, 1952 and was trained as an Air Traffic Controller. He was stationed in the Marshall Islands and was witness to several nuclear tests conducted by the US Government. Francis served four years and was medically discharged after spending a year at a military hospital in Hawaii trying to recover from his radiation exposure.

"Big Mike", codenamed "Ivy Mike", was tested on Enewetak Atoll on November 1, 1952. The United States conducted the test and it was the first full-scale test of a thermonuclear hydrogen bomb ever to take place at Bikini Atoll. Nuclear fallout poisoned the people living in the surrounding area, including the military personnel closest to the test site.

Ivy Mike (yield 10.4 mt) - an atmospheric nuclear test conducted by the U.S. at Enewetak Atoll on 1 November 1952. It was the world's first successful hydrogen bomb. Image in the public domain

At the time, it had been decided that only a full-scale test would validate the idea of the Teller-Ulam design. Ivy Mike weighed 74 metric tons and was housed in a large corrugated aluminum building. The building was 88 feet long, 46 feet wide and 61 feet high. There were a total of 9,350 military and 2,300 civilian personnel involved in the operation.[6]

While Francis did not directly witness "Big Mike", the aftermath was devastating. He was stationed in the Marshall Islands for a bomb test even larger than "Big Mike" (AKA "Ivy Mike"). The largest thermonuclear explosion tested in the Marshall Islands happened on March 1, 1954, while Francis was stationed in the

19

Marshall Islands. It was a 15 megaton explosion called Castle Bravo, 1,000 times more powerful than the bomb the US dropped on Hiroshima in 1945.[7] The fallout from the explosions rained down like snow. Sadly, some of the local children found it entertaining and played in the toxic powder, not realizing the danger.

Francis John Kelly, born September 6, 1932 was Chris' father, the youngest of four, he had two brothers and a sister. Francis' was 3 when his mother died, then his mother when he was 7. Francis and his siblings grew up under his Aunt and Uncle's care. Francis' older sister took on the burden of parenthood and helped raise him and his brothers John and Paul. They lived in Scranton, PA, the front door of their home just 100 feet from the entrance of the local coal mine.

Unfortunately, Francis' exposure to the radioactive isotopes of Ivy Mike and Castle Bravo were devastating. It also didn't help that he grew up close to a Pennsylvania coal mine that left him in poor health during his later years. Francis died of colon cancer on February 5, 2008 and Chris' mother Ruth died of pancreatic cancer in 2003.

Chris recalls his cousins stopped showing up at holidays and birthday parties. At the time he didn't realize why his family stopped socializing with his cousins and relatives. It was only later that Chris learned when Francis decided not to sue the government and when that happened, Uncle Paul broke off communication with the family; they never heard from him again. As Chris put it, "Uncle Paul was pissed that dad didn't sue."

Although more than 60 years have passed, today the Marshall Islands are 10 times more radioactive than Chernobyl. The islands are located between The Philippines and Hawaii in the south Pacific. The islands may never be inhabited by humans again.

Little Known Fact

The "bikini" worn today was not exactly named after Bikini Atoll. Competing French fashion designers Louis Reard and Jacques Heim wanted the two-piece swimsuit to be, as they put it, the swimsuit would be "explosive", just like the news-making atomic bombs tested in the Marshall Islands. Heim even called his the "atom", advertised as the world's smallest bathing suit.[8]

The Move to Syracuse

Francis' exposure to the radioactive fallout of Ivy Mike and other nuclear testing in the Marshall Islands left him suffering from a collapsed lung. Doctor's tried to operate and bring him back to full health, but they had no luck. Francis being unable to recover from his condition made him ineligible to perform his military duties. After spending nearly a year in a military hospital in Hawaii, Francis was medically discharged from the

US Airforce December 1, 1956 and had to figure out his next step.

The Jesuit Priests at Le Moyne College had a reputation for helping Veterans in the community. Francis, being a devout Catholic and Veteran in need, decided the move to Syracuse, NY, he felt it would be a good place to raise a family. Since Francis was not well-equipped to work in the furniture factory as he did before his military service, he needed an education and help in applying his skills in other, less physical ways. Going to college seemed like the best next thing to do, so Francis found a Catholic college in Syracuse, NY: Le Moyne.

The idea for Le Moyne College emerged like so many other colleges at the time. Thousands of former military men and women needed an education. The G.I. Bill, formally known as The Servicemen's Readjustment Act of 1944 created programs to help soldiers prepare for a normal life. Returning veterans were motivated to attend college, a luxury that had been denied to most of their parents.[9]

Chris' father enrolled as a student in 1956, where he met his wife Ruth Marie. They both graduated from Le Moyne College in 1960. The move to Syracuse was an important step for Francis and his future family, but he had difficulty coping with life and chose alcohol to self-medicate.

Episode 2: A Boy and His Teddy Bear...

...along with a Dad and his beer.

Francis' experience working for the government was traumatic, so in order to cope with everyday life, he self-medicated. Chris' dad was an alcoholic. Growing up with an alcoholic father wasn't easy.

Most children of alcoholics don't know what to expect from one day to the next. However, Chris could tell what kind of evening it would be by the way his dad drove up the street and how he parked in the driveway. At this point in Chris' life he was becoming conscious of the world around him and understanding what was really going on.

What's challenging about children of one or more alcoholic parents is that as they mature into adulthood, it may be difficult to develop healthy, trusting interpersonal relationships.[10] Children of alcoholics often deny their feelings of sadness, fear and anger in order to survive. But those feelings have a tendency to surface as they get older.

Favorite Son

Chris was viewed as the favorite by his siblings because his father would always invite him to run errands. "Dad would always take the back roads from our house to the local food mart to pick up his beer." During the meandering drive, Chris and his dad would talk about his experience in the Airforce. Although Chris' father would always offer to buy him candy, Chris would consistently turn the offers down, knowing how financially strapped the family was for money.

Chris was the oldest of four, so it made sense he was called upon to join dad in running errands. However, Francis had an ulterior motive. On more than one occasion, Francis would hide his beer on his hip while entering the house, knowing that Mom would be excited to see Chris and talk about their errand-running. While Chris was distracting mom by her own excitement in seeing her favorite son, his dad would quietly disappear down the narrow basement stairs. There in the basement, adjacent to the cold, granite foundation, his dad would hide so he could drink his beer. At this point Chris realized he was just a diversion to support his father's alcoholism.

As time passed, Mom started catching on to what was happening. She never said anything, but everyone sensed that something was amiss. One day, Francis announced that the house needed another exit. The construction project started almost immediately. Chris' dad dug out a hole alongside the outside of the house, adjacent to the driveway. Then, he carefully removed the necessary granite blocks to install a doorway. Mom and Chris realized what was happening, Francis was finding a way to separate himself from the family and avoid conflict while drinking.

Francis installed what is commonly referred to as a "Dutch Door", which is a single door that is horizontally split at the center. This allowed the top of the door to remain open for ventilation while the bottom of the door stayed closed. The Dutch Door let a little light and air into the basement and prevented the family dog from escaping. Soon, Chris and his Dad no longer entered the house through the front door. Chris would still come in the front door to greet and distract his mom, but Francis would immediately escape to his basement bunker through the newly built side entrance to enjoy his beer in private.

Family and Siblings

Chris was the oldest of four with 11 years between him and his youngest sibling. Mom and Dad (Francis) tried having more children after Chris was born, but experienced several miscarriages. When Chris was in Elementary School, his newly adopted sister Kate entered his life. Chris was so excited to have a sister he begged his parents to bring her into school for show-and-tell. After Kate (Katherine) came his sister Mary, who Grandma nicknamed "Marnie" when she was just a few weeks old. Next was Ann and then a couple years later brother Jon was born.

Jon was a preemie. Chris recalls his tiny head being smaller than the palm of his mother's hand. Mom and Jon were in and out of the hospital four months before mom and Jon were finally safe at home. Like many women giving birth, mom ended up with blood clots in her arms and legs and the doctors wanted to make sure she would be okay.

Kindergarten

The first day of kindergarten Chris didn't know where he was going and his mom recanted this story often. Chris was dropped off at the front of the school like all the other kids, he walked into a classroom with small tables and chairs sitting with his new friends. All the kids were turning around waving to their mothers, sobbing; many leaving their babies for the first time for such a long period of time. Chris just kept walking and never looked back. This really upset Chris' mom. As he explained to her later in life, "It wasn't personal mom, I just knew I had to do what was expected of me."

Summer after Second Grade

Most students get to enjoy what feels like a short summer playing outside with their friends and enjoying the mischief that kids get into when parents aren't around. It seemed like any other day when Chris woke up that morning, but he felt a little funny. He pleaded with his mom to stay inside, but like all parents at the time, Chris was ushered out the door and told to go play and come back to get something to eat at lunchtime.

Chris came back well before lunch. He could see the look of disappointment in mom's face, then he saw fright. Chris was ill. He was rushed to the hospital and didn't leave for two months.

The best Chris can recall, he looked like Violet from the movie *Charlie and The Chocolate Factory*. He had green, yellow and purple dots all over his body. The doctors were puzzled. They would stop by to examine him, poking and prodding and asking if anything hurt. Although Francis was still alive, Chris' first thought at the time was that he must have what his father has and would probably get sick and die of cancer before going back to school. He spent a lot of time contemplating his longevity.

Chris spent the entire time he was hospitalized in one position. He was restrained in his bed, doctors and nurses kept telling him to be still. Chris had two intravenous tubes, one in each arm and all he could do was lay there with nothing solid to eat.

Fortunately, Mom and Dad brought a 12-inch color television into his room. That was a big deal at the time and those TVs probably weighed 30 pounds.

The nurse would ask what Chris wanted to watch. All Chris wanted to watch was *Captain Kangaroo*, but the nurse could never find the channel, so he had to watch *Romper Room*. During the beginning of every *Romper Room* episode, the host would be looking through her magic mirror and in Chris' opinion, she would be creepily staring through the screen at her viewers saying she could "see" you. During her opening monologue, she would call out common children's names, but she never mentioned Chris; she never saw him. This made Chris very irritated. Maybe if she saw him, Chris thought, she would be able to send help? Maybe the magic mirror could figure out what was wrong with Chris? But that never happened.

Chris remembers the G-men visiting him in the hospital and saying they were going to send a team to check the backyard where he was last playing before falling ill. Chris never learned what ailed him, but the spots went away and he finally went home. He got to spend a few weeks in the house before school started.

When Chris went back to school to start the 3rd grade the teacher asked all the students to write down what they did during their summer vacation. Since Chris spent the summer in the hospital hooked up to IV's, he chose not to participate. He recalls at the time, "How do you explain something when you don't know what it is? How do you explain to a group of third-graders what it was like to be a prisoner?"

The best part of the ordeal Chris can recall is that there was no fighting between Mom and Dad. Since the G-men came to visit, maybe it had something to do with Dad? If it did, it seems that the government must have paid for everything because in Chris' opinion, a hospital bill after a two-month stay would have bankrupted his parents.

Racism is Stupid

In third grade science class Chris first learned about prisms and how they refracted the color of light. He realized in this moment that racism was stupid. Chris decided that the white man is only reflecting the color white, but was actually a combination of all colors combined into one body. It was his deep thinking that made him realize that school wasn't fast enough for him. Chris found his mind wandering often, but would eventually slow his mind down by introducing a physical tiredness from sports and playing outside with the neighborhood kids.

Windows Open

Chris enjoyed having friends over, but never had a sleepover because he never knew when his parents would get into a fight. The fighting always seemed to be about money. Since Francis was in sales his income was a combination of salary and commission. It seems that when the commission checks were coming in, everything was alright. But when commissions were lower than normal that month and dad was drinking, the fights would start.

Chris lived in a working-class neighborhood just outside of Syracuse, NY. All the neighborhood kids would come by to play. No one had air conditioning, which meant in the summer time the windows would be open to let in the cool breezes flowing across the Great Lakes and down from the Adirondacks. But it also meant your family's business was flowing out of the windows for all the neighbors to hear.

Some of the older kids eventually became Chris' babysitters. Chris enjoyed his parents being the "hip" couple in the neighborhood, because all the kids would come to play in the yard. Most of the neighbors were what you would expect in a tightly-knit Roman Catholic community, but not all of his neighbors made good decisions.

Dad the Hero

At nine years old, Chris recalls the parents of the family across the street went out of town. The older kids in the house decided to host a "glue party". The smell of the glue party was noxious. Sniffing glue was one way that teenagers would get a low-cost high those days. People that use inhalants or have become addicted to glue sniffing, paint, or other chemicals report a temporary sense of euphoria. In some cases, addicts reportedly experience hallucinations.[11] Since the high is so temporary, these glue parties required all the windows and doors be sealed for the party to start. But it also created a dangerous situation for its participants. Aside from the smell, Chris recalls most memorably his parents panicking and worrying the family would come home to a house full of dead teenagers. Chris remembers his mom calling for help and then his dad assisting the police in breaking down the door and getting the teenagers to safety. As he recalls from this situation, Chris realized that he would also speak up and do the right thing when the situation called for it.

Speaking Up

It's usually not easy for children to speak up for themselves. It is sometimes even more difficult for students in a classroom setting to do what is considered, "talking back" to your teachers. The teachers at Chris' school tolerated his behavior because he was intellectually mature for his age. In retrospect, perhaps since Chris was speaking up for himself at such an early age could have been a sign that something special about Chris required more attention.

In talking to Chris it seems this is one of his first memories where he believes his bipolar condition began to surface. Chris didn't feel that respectfully disagreeing with an adult was an issue. But he soon realized that most students did not speak up for themselves, even when the teacher was wrong.

Chris didn't let his young age deter him from speaking his mind in a respectful manner. He recalls one incident in 7th grade while sitting in Sister Mary Joy's class. Chris' friend Pat was disturbing him. It got to the point where Chris yelled, "Cut it out!" and was told by Sister Mary Joy he had to leave and go immediately to the principal's office. Most students would have complied by walking to the principal's office, perhaps a phone call or a note home would have been pinned to his winter jacket, but not Chris.

Chris decided he would stand his ground and instead engaged the teacher in an intellectual conversation about the matter, "If you want to go to the principal's office you can, but I'm here to learn." Chris never left his chair and Sister Mary Joy finished teaching the class. After the bell rang to change classes, Chris and Sister Mary Joy went their separate ways and never talked about the incident again. Chris believes that his unusual height helped him to stand his ground on more than one occasion. Being tall commanded a certain level of respect that other students were not receiving from the school's teachers.

School Daze / Church Service

In 6th and 7th grade Chris shot up in height and was the one of the tallest kids in his class. He was already an altar boy and given his height, he was a natural selection to be the one that carried the Crucifix. Carrying the Crucifix is a big deal as a Roman Catholic altar boy. This meant you were the first person into the church, leading the Entrance Procession with the Deacons and Eucharistic Ministers walking past the parishioners already in their pews. The Priest celebrating the mass is typically the last person to reach the altar. The Crucifix itself is usually five feet tall and weighing at least 20 pounds, so being tall and strong had its advantages.

There are many benefits of becoming an altar boy (or altar girl). One such benefit from the Roman Catholic Church's perspective is to garner interest in youngsters to consider a career in the church. Although Chris had considered the priesthood at one point in his early years, he most fondly remembered the relationship he had with Bishop Harrison.

Bishop Harrison (1912-2004) was born in Syracuse NY and was one of six children. He graduated from St. Lucy Academy, where he was class president and valedictorian. Before joining the priesthood and earning his way to one of the highest positions in the Catholic Church, Francis James Harrison graduated from Notre Dame.[12] Bishop Harrison was quite fond of his college alma mater, and best friends with its sitting president, Theodore M. Hesburgh, C.S.C., who served as president of Notre Dame for 35 years, from 1987-2005.[13]

Chris didn't realize it at the time, but his church was probably one of the most progressive of its time. While other Roman Catholic masses being held across the country were extremely formal, St. James Church in Syracuse NY was much more relaxed. During mass, Bishop Harrison would say, "Hey Chris, go find out the score of the Notre Dame game". Chris would take off running for the rectory, which was approximately the length of one loop around a 400 meter track. Parishioners probably thought Father Harrison sent Chris on an important errand, or maybe they ran out of hosts for the Communion Sacrament. One progressive priest even organized trips for the kids that played youth basketball. Chris recalls one trip in particular that held a different meaning to him as he got older and realized what was really happening.

Visit to NYC

Chris played Catholic Youth Organization (CYO) basketball. The CYO organized sports for the local parish where Chris grew up. Along with sports, the church would also organize trips to local sporting events and museums. Some trips were more sports related, like skating and skiing. The CYO ran sports programs in the summer to keep the kids busy and give their parents a break.

During Chris' freshman year, a trip for the CYO was organized by one of the more progressive priests in the parish. Father Ahern became a priest later in life. He didn't follow the normal path of lifelong students of the Bible. Chris described him as focused, funny and hip.

New York City was supposed to have the best pizza in the state. Father Ahern insisted the students visit a pizza place he knew of in Greenwich Village where they would also meet up with a friend of the priest. Little did Chris know, that isn't all they would meet.

Father Ahern reminded Chris of the character from the television hit M.A.S.H. Specifically, Hawkeye Pierce, with his sledgehammer wit and biting sarcastic words. It was fun to be around him according to Chris because he talked to you like a normal person.

While waiting for Father Ahern's friend to arrive the boys were mostly standing around taking in all the sights. There were lots of people-watching to be done. Chris was enjoying the new sights and smells when a young woman approached him and asked Chris how he was doing. Chris smiled, "I'm doing fine, how are you." She smiled and said, "I'll do anything for $8." Immediately, Chris was thinking, maybe she would come back to Syracuse and clean his room. Chris smiled at the thought of having a personal maid. Then, she said, "Okay, I can see you're thinking about it, how about $5?"

Chris could see that Father Ahern was watching the situation unfold. Chris then started putting everything together. The girl that approached him had long straight hair, a porkpie hat, oversized hoop earrings and platform-heeled shoes. Chris then realized, she was definitely...a prostitute...and he was being propositioned. But it wasn't in this moment that realization surfaced. Father Ahern never said anything and neither did Chris, and the girl eventually walked away.

Several years later when Chris saw the movie Taxi Driver with Robert De Niro. It was Jodie Foster's character that reminded Chris of the girl that propositioned him years earlier. She wasn't interested in cleaning his room after all. Chris remembers saying it out loud, "She was a prostitute," while watching the movie. His buddy corrected him and told Chris, "No, she IS a prostitute." Then Chris told him the story of his CYO visit to Greenwich Village and they both had a good laugh.

The next week became a historic moment in NYC history. During the evening of July 13, 1977 the city lost power and didn't get it restored for over 24 hours. The Mets were forced to stop their baseball game in the sixth inning against the Chicago Cubs. Some parts of the city experienced rioting, arson and looting.[14] Chris was thankful his visit was the prior week. It was then that Chris realized that he liked road trips and visiting new places.

Boys Road Trip

Cousin Jack was a student at Notre Dame in 1975. Dad and
Uncle Paul thought it would be a fun road trip to catch the last
football game of the season. The drive from Syracuse, New
York to South Bend, Indiana was almost 10 hours along the
south side of Lake Ontario. Francis and Paul took turns driving
while Chris and his cousin found ways to entertain themselves
playing license plate bingo and seeing who could add up all the
numbers on the license plates the fastest.

While Chris didn't share the same enthusiasm for football as
Bishop Harrison, he did get to witness history in the making.
Cousin Jack was able to get five seats in the student section,
which was behind the goal posts and above the tunnel where
the players entered the field. The game Chris watched was a
thrill! The sound of the crowd was so loud it was deafening. He
remembers he could feel the percussion from the crowd's
cheering in his chest. While Chris didn't learn of the importance
of the back story of this Notre Dame vs Georgia Tech game, he
is able to now reflect on its importance.

The game Chris and family witnessed was made popular by
Hollywood decades later. Daniel "Rudy" Ruettiger, class of
1976 was a hard-working defensive lineman. He showed up for
every practice anticipating he would get the playing time he had
earned. Although he only stood at 5'6", he played with the
intensity and determination of anyone else on the squad. Rudy

earned a spot on the scout team, the team that helped the varsity team practice for games. Despite his work ethic, he didn't play a single down during the regular season. The last play of the November 8, 1975 game against Georgia Tech (GT), Rudy was activated as a defensive end and sacked the quarterback from GT, Rudy Allen.[15]

Chris couldn't understand why Rudy was carried off the field by his teammates. It wasn't something that normally happened while watching other football games. But as Chris later learned, perseverance and determination are keys to getting noticed and realizing your dreams. While Chris considered Notre Dame, given its affiliation with the Catholic Church, Chris would attend elsewhere when the time came to make that decision.

When Chris asked his cousin why he was going to college, the reply was simple: "You need to go to college to earn money", Chris recalls. "I was already earning money at the time" Chris said during an interview one day, "...but I realized I couldn't deliver newspapers my whole life and there weren't enough people dying for me to make more than $20 every few weeks...besides that, who wants to see a 6' tall twenty-something year old altar boy?" Chris chuckled.

Earning Money

Chris didn't realize it, but his service as an altar boy helped him earn some money. One afternoon, Chris was called to the Rectory[16] and learned of his first opportunity to serve outside the church. He accepted an opportunity to serve as altar boy at a funeral. After losing a loved one, some families have a full mass before traveling to the funeral home while other families skip the formal church setting and have an abbreviated mass at the funeral home with the local parish priest and altar staff.

At Chris' first funeral serving as an Altar Boy, the director gave him a $20 tip. From that day forward, every time a funeral was taking place at St. James, Chris got out of school for an hour and made $20. Chris was also invited to support all of the high-visibility masses like Palm Sunday, Easter, Midnight mass on Christmas Eve. Chris still chuckles about the situation to this day...imagine making $20 in the early 70's while all your friends are sitting in school? Chris never said a word to the funeral director about the $20, and the funeral director never said a word to Chris. All Chris could take away from this situation is that when you're working and doing a good job, you make money.

Newspapers: Not Always Black and White

Chris' love for earning money helped him realize something: why did Mom and dad have a paperboy deliver a paper to the house every day when Chris could do that job? So in 7th grade Chris took on a paper route. He started out The *Herald-Journal* with 90 customers.

The Herald Journal was a daily newspaper. You were supposed to be 12, but since Chris was so tall, the paper let Chris take the paper over from his friend Sammy Padavona. Sammy was related to heavy metal front man Ronny James Dio ("Dio" meaning "God" in Italian), famous for working with several bands including Rainbow, Black Sabbath and then his solo career band just called "Dio."[17]

Chris made good money during the paper route. It was great exercise and gave Chris something to do after school. When the owner of the district Mr. Hamilton died, his wife came to the house to share the sad news. Chris was worried this would cause a problem with his paper route, but his mom helped Chris understand that papers still had to be delivered because people would want to be informed. This gave Chris a bigger idea: he convinced his Mom to buy part of the paper route for the Valley Drive section of The *Herald-Journal*. Mom made an initial investment with the district; then within two years, she bought the rest of the Valley District.

Chris thought this was another opportunity. Since the fighting between Francis and Mom were usually about money, maybe the fights would go away? Chris worried that maybe the fights weren't just about money, so Chris tried to convince mom to leave his father so the family could have sanctuary in the house, but that negotiation failed.

The *Post Standard* was founded in 1929 as The *Onondaga Standard*. Syracuse had a population of 135,000 by 1900. In 1939, publisher Samuel I. Newhouse acquired the market's two evening papers. Times changed and people's information and news habits changed as well. By the end of the 20th century the appetite for two newspapers had disappeared. The *Herald-Journal* closed in 2001 and was made part of a paper called *The Post-Standard.* [18]

Over time, the newspaper started taking distribution districts back from the families that ran the districts like a franchise. The Newhouse organization knew families would have to go to court to reclaim their districts they had worked for so many years. But the families that ran these franchises didn't have the money to battle the wrongdoing in court, so it was easier just to give them up and find another way to make a living.

As Chris reflected back on this period he asked, "How could anyone fight what was going on? Who were you going to call and complain, the newspapers?" Since the newspaper controlled the information they would never allow a story like that to be published. In Chris' opinion, The Newhouse organization stole money from honest, hardworking families by forcing them to give up their districts.

Solomon Newhouse and his family ran one of the largest media organizations in U.S. History. By 1916, at the age of 21, Newhouse was earning $30,000 per year. In the early 1920s he started acquiring failing newspapers and making them profitable. By the time of his death in 1979, Newhouse was the third largest newspaper chain in the United States. The organization's assets included 31 newspapers, 15 cable television systems, 7 magazines, 6 television stations and 5 radio stations. Syracuse University was able to establish the Newhouse School of Public Communications thanks to his generous $15 million donation.[19]

It was during the 8th grade that Chris started to notice the opposite sex. Perfectly natural for boys and girls at this age. Since Chris was earning decent money at the time, it only made sense that he start dating.

Attraction and Confusion

Chris was a devout Roman Catholic. By 8th grade, Chris had thoughts about becoming a priest, but wasn't sure. It was a confusing time for Chris, so much happening socially and emotionally. He was always attracted to the opposite sex, and finally built up the courage to ask a girl out on a date, Linda.

In 8th grade, Chris was the tallest kid in the school, standing at almost 5'11". Chris asked Linda to go out on a date with him, and she said "yes"; Chris was thrilled. Most boys Chris' age practice being rejected more than being accepted, so it was a special moment in his emotional maturity.

Although Chris lived in a large city, the Roman Catholic community was tight-knit, everyone knew everyone and sometimes, inappropriately got into each other's business. Just a few days after asking Linda out, Chris was on his way up to his house through the driveway after walking home from school, she didn't look happy. He remembers mom stopping him in the middle of the driveway, this couldn't be good he thought to himself. Mom said she just got off the phone with someone from the school and said they didn't want Chris to date Linda because they thought it was a problem. As Chris puts it, "I lost my sexual innocence right there." Chris tried to figure out why someone wouldn't want him and Linda to date. He was crushed.

Chris started thinking about the worst thing that could happen if the two of them started dating and mentally worked his way back from that moment when he asked Linda out, to the news spreading, to the gossip and opinion that followed, to standing in the driveway getting emotionally crushed by his Mom's words. Chris deduced that someone must have been worried that Linda and Chris would start having pre-marital sex; then they would be guilty of violating the teachings of the bible.

The situation was very confusing and upsetting for Chris. He wasn't sure if he wanted to yell, cry, or throw bricks through the school's windows. As Chris wrestled with his feelings, he realized that emotions can prompt people to do things, but he kept his emotions in check and reflected in that moment that if everyone acted on their emotions all the time, society would be a complete mess.

Teddy Bears Can Become Grizzlies

The situation where the adults decided what was best for Chris and Linda was upsetting. This didn't make Chris angry, but what did make Chris angry was being woken up from sleep. The family learned that sleeping bears should be left alone.

Chris used to take naps after school. He used to fall asleep on the living room carpet, hardwood flooring, the varnished decorative brick around the fireplace, it didn't make a difference. When Chris needed a nap, he took a nap. He would take his nap wherever and whenever he felt tired.

Chris and younger brother Jon shared a bedroom. One afternoon Chris made it to his bed to take in his after-school nap. It felt like moments had passed when Mom wanted Chris to wake up. She sent Jon to wake up his big brother. Jon was more than excited to get his big brother's attention. He was maybe 3 years old at the time and very enthusiastic. Jon crawled up on top of Chris, while sitting on him and shaking his forearm and said, "Mommy said get out of bed." Chris woke abruptly, picked up tiny Jon and threw him over to his own bed. Jon wasn't hurt, and probably didn't mind flying for the first time. Jon didn't mind poking the bear. After all, it was his big brother.

Being the big brother of the family came with certain responsibilities. As Chris recalls, his mom made sure Chris understood that she had expectations of him being the oldest. The rules were simple...all he had to do was follow them.

School Rules

Freshman year in high school mom came to Chris and said "I trust you and you, and I have one rule: you need to get good grades in school." Chris had no curfew and could do pretty much anything he wanted because he was so much older than his brothers and sisters. Chris was a good student and always kept up his grades, which landed him an academic scholarship to college, we'll get to that later.

As long as Chris' siblings didn't find out he was up late or out late with his friends, mom would let things slide. Chris realized Moms are inherently smart, because her one rule was actually two rules. The only way to get good grades in school is to show up, so there were actually two rules. Chris never went back and corrected his mom, but instead, appreciated the fact that if a rule is written well and abided by those following, sometimes there could be three or four other rules or conditions that had to be followed in order to succeed. That was okay with Chris because he liked school. School gave Chris the opportunity to learn and play sports - two of his favorite pastimes.

Being an Athlete can be Painful

Chris went to Christian Brothers Academy for High School. Tim Downs was one of Chris' best friends growing up. Tim told Chris that football sign-ups were soon and camp was going to start. Spring Valley NY was the location of the football camp. Chris didn't bring a razor to camp and by the end of the week of practice Chris had his first beard.   Practices were double-sessions: a practice in the morning and a practice in the evening. Since camp was in the valley in late summer, it was nice and cool. During the cool summer mornings the fog was thick and the air was still. The athletes could never really see how far they were running because of the lack of visibility from the heavy mist and density of the fog. While running Chris recalls the heavy mist lapping on his cheeks and making his hair and clothing damp and heavy with each stride. The mist was dense enough to form tiny droplets on his arms hairs. With all that heat and moisture, football camp is also where Chris first contracted Athletes foot.

Athlete's foot is exactly how it sounds. It can be contracted by another athlete or developed from bacteria left unattended inside the warm, moist, tightly fitting sneaker, shoe, or skate of its victim. The itching burning rash can last several days or weeks. If left untreated, the infection can spread to the toenails. It earned its rightful name because it is mostly seen in athletes.

Chris' feet were so bad they looked like swollen pink sponges. Traditional medicines weren't working, so Chris treated his condition with bleach. This condition left Chris quite irritable. In order to be successful in football it probably helped to be irritable, but not all the time.

Although every athlete recalls the one or two "hated" teams they had to face, sometimes players that practiced against each other developed the same level of animosity. For some reason Michael Redfern had it in for Chris. Maybe something happened during football camp, but Chris can't really remember.

Brawl in the Hall

All Chris remembers is that Michael used to start fights with him on a regular basis, on the field and off. Chris was never the type of person to start or look for a fight, but he knew he had to protect himself when necessary. Since football is a game of violent collisions, it was only a matter of time before players would take it personally. What more would one expect from a testosterone-filled teenager with an attitude and a grudge?

One morning in the hallway at school Michael gave Chris a look and started moving towards him like he was going to attack, so Chris attacked first. The skirmish lasted about 30 seconds before a homeroom teacher in front of his classroom door ran down the hall to break up the fight.

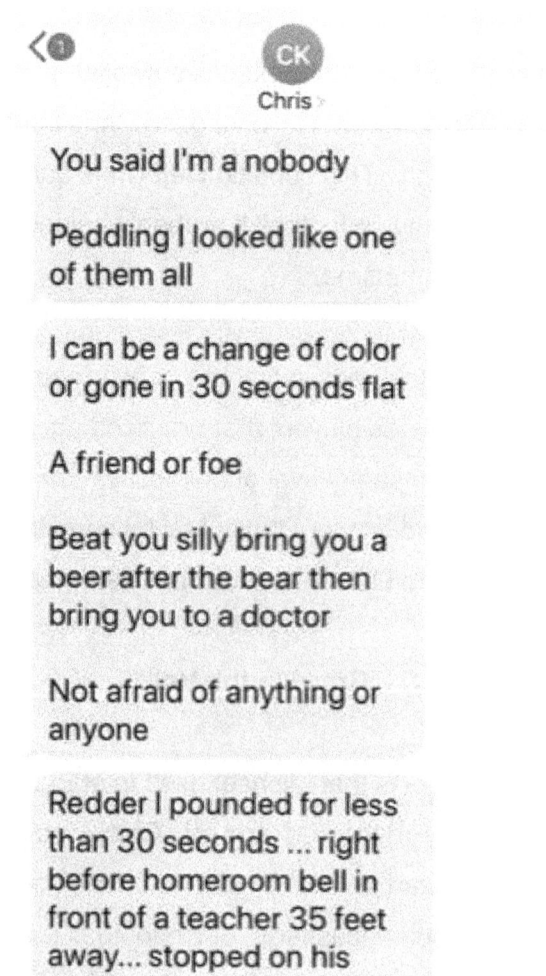

Chris

You said I'm a nobody

Peddling I looked like one of them all

I can be a change of color or gone in 30 seconds flat

A friend or foe

Beat you silly bring you a beer after the bear then bring you to a doctor

Not afraid of anything or anyone

Redder I pounded for less than 30 seconds ... right before homeroom bell in front of a teacher 35 feet away... stopped on his

command went into
homeroom read bibble
dribble verse.. who is it
against... versus who?
went to first class called to
office told off vp walked
out I was over it... saw
redder he was tattered...
maybe too much...
balanced out not real rules
in fights... three attacks
and same look before
attacks... justified 100%...

Who said you're a
nobody?

Reffer

There were two Chris Kelly's in the school at the time, so on the
loudspeaker "freshman" was included in the announcement for
him to come to the principal's office.

Chris was told while sitting in the principal's office that he was
suspended for five days. Chris told the principal, "You asked
me no questions, so you can't judge me fairly." Chris walked
back to class and sat back in his seat and attended class for the
next week as if nothing had happened. Chris never served the
suspension and never heard anything again.

Chris didn't realize it at the time, but Bipolar Disorder can lead
to not only verbal but physical aggression. Some even refer to

it as "bipolar rage". A research study uncovered that over 87% of subjects in the study with Bipolar Disorder reported notably higher aggression scores than study participants without the disorder.[20]

What Chris has learned is there are certain "triggers" that move him emotionally from a stable to a more aggressive state. As he recognizes this shift in his emotions, Chris takes a step back and observes the situation from outside of his body and becomes a coach to himself. Instead of acting impulsively, Chris counteracts what could be seen as verbal or physical aggression by first realizing the trigger that has presented itself and then making a conscious effort to behave in an appropriate and socially acceptable manner. Without his diagnosis and therapy, he would not have been aware of why he was acting or speaking out. Although Chris struggled a little with his physical acting out, his intellectual prowess earned him a full college scholarship to Rochester Institute of Technology.

College

Chris entered college at the age of 17. He was young enough to be able to continue playing youth hockey but wanted to focus on his studies (more about Chris playing hockey in Episode 10...remember...this book isn't in chronological order ☺). Chris entered Rochester Institute of Technology (RIT) where he studied programming and computer systems on an academic scholarship.

College had its challenges for Chris, his unbeknownst bipolar condition was driving him crazy. Along with the bouts of mania and depression, Chris was learning a great deal of new information about computers and the future. At this point in Chris' studies he started to realize that George Orwell's book *1984* was more like a blueprint for how society would change and humans would become slaves to technology. Like all evolution, Chris could see a slow, incremental dependency on computers. His fear was at some point in the future, humans would no longer be in control. This newly discovered knowledge was giving Chris nightmares regularly.

RIT had trimesters. The second two trimesters Chris made Dean's list with a perfect 5.0, mom was very proud because she knew Chris was still following her two rules she bestowed upon him early in life, he was going to class and proving his knowledge. Chris went back to college in September and within days of returning he recalls having a conversation with his mom, and all she said was "Dad lost his job...we'll figure it out." Chris decided to go home because he knew he was more valuable at home helping out the family, plus, he could not deal with everything going on.

Decision-making can be an issue for people suffering from Bipolar Disorder. The mood swings that accompany the disorder can cloud one's judgement. This, coupled with the potential for impulsive behavior helps Chris make sense of this moment in his life. Given all the stress piled on top of Chris at this moment in his life, he could have been experiencing a manic period without knowing it. Chris would never go back to school. The consequences of this decision would limit Chris' opportunities in the future, but this is symptomatic of someone who is Bipolar.

Chris went home because he knew Dad was going to be trouble for the family. Chris was also struggling emotionally with his undiagnosed bipolar condition, but didn't really understand why his mind wasn't working the way it used to. As Chris reflected on the changes in his life during this time period he realized that exercise was his medication. He had stopped playing sports when he entered University. Looking back, Chris realizes that intense physical activity helped suppress his condition and triggers.

It's been well documented that exercise causes pain, but when the body experiences pain it naturally releases endorphins to counteract what the body is feeling. The feeling can even be euphoric and some research papers have even confirmed the experience can be similar to the highly addictive drugs morphine or codeine. Since Chris was no longer exercising and instead focusing on his studies, he believes this helped reveal his sleeping bipolar condition, which was kept below the surface of his everyday life because of his physical activity.

Chris' decision to come home was impulsive. He had several other siblings at home more than capable of helping Mom deal with dad. But in this situation, Chris allowed his triggers to take over. People with bipolar disorder are known to act on impulse. We all have urges, but most of us don't act on them immediately because we have them under control, and we are aware of the physical or social consequences for our behavior. For someone with bipolar disorder, the ability to suppress reaction to tense and emotionally triggering situations is much more difficult.

According to the International Society for Research on Impulsivity (you didn't even know they existed, did you?), the results of the original study by Whiteside and Lynam in 2001 led to a scale of impulsivity describing four traits:

1. **Negative Urgency**: tendency to act rashly under extreme negative conditions
2. **Lack of Premeditation**: tendency to act without thinking
3. **Lack of Perseverance**: inability to remain focused on a task
4. **Sensation Seeking**: tendency to seek out novel and thrilling experiences[21]

The first few weeks living at home were a big adjustment for Chris. He was used to having his freedom and he was only responsible for himself. It took some adjustment. As Chris reflects back on this moment, he realizes now his bipolar disorder had him triggered into believing home was going to be a disaster and only when he stepped in to help his mom would things normalize.

But a few weeks later after moving back into his old room with Jon, it wasn't as bad as he thought it would be. Francis built a pool for the kids to use in the summer months and Chris would play the role of lifeguard, occasionally cooling his feet by the edge of the pool. If any of the kids looked like they were in trouble all Chris had to do is walk in and pluck them out of the water, like the giant in the story Gulliver's Travels.

Chris didn't mind living in Syracuse, but the more time he spent there as an adult, the more he realized he would like to move somewhere warm. Chris and his sweetheart Laura spent a little time in Syracuse after being married, but both agreed it would be nice to live someplace warmer.

Episode 3: Not Always Sunny in Florida

Syracuse NY is one of the cloudiest cities in the country. Some say the city has more "rain days" than rain because of the gray skies and ongoing drizzle starting in the fall. During November and December the sun only finds its way through the clouds less than one-third of the time between sunrise and sunset. It's understandable why someone would yearn for sunshine and warmer weather.

The "lake effect" is one of the reasons Syracuse is gray. Located due southeast of Lake Ontario, prevailing winds from the west and north blow across the surface of the lake, which picks up moisture that forms cloud banks across the land. Then, as the clouds rise to drift above the foothills of the Adirondack mountains, a slow, steady drizzle is released. After the clouds have expelled enough liquid, they are able to drift to their destination.

In the late 80's Chris and his sweetheart Laura were married and set their sights on Florida. They both wanted better weather and a nicer atmosphere. What better state than "The Sunshine State", the tagline emblazoned under most license plates in the state of Florida. On average, Florida has 237 days of sunshine each year, which beats the U.S. average of 205 sunshine days by just over 15%.[22]

Laura was an older woman, by two years. A German girl with blonde hair and blue eyes with a gymnasts body. In Chris' opinion, he describes her as being, "Cute as a button, but a pain in the ass."

While in Florida, Chris expanded his career in the newspaper industry: not delivering papers, but on the production side. Although a dying medium of information today, newspapers were once the primary source of information. Journalists wrote articles based on sources and typically had to corroborate their stories with at least three sources. Chris worked for three major papers, Florida Today, USA Today and Investor's Business Daily.

Florida Today was initially called "TODAY" and was created to compete with the regional Orlando Sentinel and state-wide Miami Herald. The Gannett Corporation started the paper in the late 60's. Papers were delivered at no cost to readers in Brevard County for its first two weeks in operation. This move guaranteed the minimum circulation requirements set by its advertisers.[23]

During his print media career, Chris held 12 different jobs and started out as a paper boy. While working the night shift, he was in charge of scanning content, photographs, plates and overseeing a small team of technicians. Most newspapers are printed between midnight and 2:00 am so it can include the breaking news late in the evening or early morning hours. High-speed presses print as many papers as the market demands, so the newspaper print offices are strategically located to serve a metropolitan area.

The newspaper production process can be broken into four segments: 1) Content Gathering, 2) Pre-Press, 3) Press, and 4) Post Press. Chris spent his time in segments two and three respectively. Given his ability to multitask and success in overseeing his technical team, he became the manager of the night shift.

During "Pre Press", Chris would oversee scanning, photographs, and the preparation of plates. As Chris quickly learned, he was actually the last "editor" in the process before the words would permanently burn to the thin paper that would be read by hundreds of thousands in the metropolitan area. If a negative was missing a letter, Chris would be launched into action. He would work his process to ensure that by the time the typesetter was fired up he had to remove a word or add a letter, burn a new plate, then get the plate in place so their reading audience wouldn't find any typos.

In the newspaper industry each page of a newspaper is created on a plate. The "plate" is a thin sheet of aluminum that has the image of the page to be printed. These plates were highly collectible at one time. During the brief 24-hour lifecycle of a newspaper, the plate is critical in the production of the newspaper.[24]

Each plate is wrapped around a large roller on the printing press with multiple sections of plates rolling to print multiple pages. The image of the plate is then burned and transferred to the sheet of newspaper. Before the plate was ready for print, Chris would need to make last-second adjustments as requested.

The newspaper industry is built on trust. The trust granted by the readers comes in two forms: 1) The information must be credible and 2) The information must be conveyed without typos. Every typo caught by a reader would erode the credibility of the paper and put people's jobs at risk.

Aluminum plates are almost obsolete, except in markets where the technology has not been adopted for cost or logistical reasons. Most newspapers around the world have found ways to eliminate the plate-making process altogether, allowing the human interface with computers. With the touch of a button, newspapers are now printing thousands of copies on laser printers as large as buildings.

Chris was so busy these days it was easy to ignore the symptoms that had created challenges for him in the past, but that was about to change.

Cloudy skies follow

While things were going well for Chris at work, his home life was eroding. Chris and Laura had only been married for almost two years: they were six days shy of their anniversary. Chris realized something had to be done to improve their situation, or one of them would end up dead.

Laura would stay out drinking most days of the week. She was a violent alcoholic. Laura would come home after a night of drinking and wake Chris from a sound sleep to talk of her evening's escapades. But if she came home and found Chris awake on the couch watching television, she would barge in after a full day and night of drinking and tell him to "fuck off", and then not want to talk to him.

One evening in the summer of 1989, Laura came home in a particularly foul drunken mood. She started hitting Chris, but Chris was running out of places to evade her attacks in the apartment. He knew the noise would be reported by the neighbors, but Laura gave him all the justification to call the police after threatening to shoot him with her handgun, a medium-sized 9mm Beretta that fit neatly in her hand. The situation calmed a bit after threatening to call the police, but the flames of animosity were only embers and would soon be fanned to a point of white-hot conflict. It was only a matter of time before things between Chris and Laura got worse.

Under Attack

A few weeks later Chris found himself in a similar situation. Chris was in the common area of the apartment, reading the rental section of the paper, looking at beach rentals and thinking maybe some time away from the apartment together. His goal was to help spend some alone time together, thinking it would help their relationship. But this evening didn't end the way Chris had imagined.

This time, Laura was demonstrably belligerent. Punching Chris repeatedly and then trying to remember where she left her handgun. Chris called the police eight times to come to his aide. The best Chris can recall is the responding officers seemed very agitated with him and kept telling Chris to calm down. It took a while to register what was going on, and Chris finally told the responding officers, "I'm the one who called for help, not her! I'm the one that called for your help, I'm the one being attacked!"

The officer in charge reminded Laura and Chris the police had received eight calls before their arrival. At the time of the incident, when police responded to domestic violence calls, 99% of the time it was the woman who called the police about a male attacker. It's likely the dispatcher requested the closest patrol car to respond to a domestic violence call, but with no mention of the caller or gender of the attacker or victim. It was easy for the responding officers to make assumptions based on past experience. Whenever we use past experience in a present situation, it's called "Unconscious Bias".

The lesson Chris learned from this episode: No matter what you think another person knows, bring them up to speed on the full context of the situation. Make no assumptions.

The police officer said, "The next time we have to come here you are both going to jail." Chris turned to Laura and said, "You better behave, or next time we are both going to jail."

The police left, but Chris still didn't feel safe. Within the hour Chris had contemplated his next move in order to stay safe and get himself out of harm's way.

"That's it, I'm out of here! I don't care if I have to sleep on the beach, anything will be better than staying here!"

Chris called a friend with a pickup truck and moved out that evening with nowhere to go. All of his belongings in the back of a pickup truck. Chris slept on the beach that night. He felt safer with no shelter than the shelter where he was under attack. The sound of the waves calmly lapping against the shoreline was just the peace and tranquility Chris needed for just one evening.

Fortunately, the newspaper business was booming and had great benefits. While Chris had filed for divorce, he had no intention of going back. However, as a student of life, he was eager to learn what went wrong in his relationship with Laura, so he sought counseling. Chris realized counseling would not repair things, but he was able to convince Laura to join him so the two of them could create their own paths in life after divorce.

During the counseling process Laura learned she was borderline "antisocial." Clinically, she would have been diagnosed with Antisocial Personality Disorder (APD). This explained a lot. People with APD typically have a low moral conscience and lack empathy for others. Some of the behaviors typically associated with APD include:

- Aggression
- Impulsivity
- Violation of the rights of others
- Pattern of disregard for the feelings of others
- Intimidation
- Violence[25]

Irresponsibility is a core attribute of people with APD. During their negative, impulsive episodes, people with APD fail to consider others and have a wanton disregard for the consequences of their actions. Their hostility towards others is usually unprovoked. These individuals are often prone to substance abuse, and in this case, Laura was a violent alcoholic, which didn't help the situation for Chris or their marriage.

This diagnosis helped Chris make sense of the world he was exiting after divorce and helped him see that he was a survivor after being in this relationship. In Chris' opinion, he described his relationship with Laura as one of parasitic manipulation. She spent her time making Chris feel bad about himself, providing Chris with a moral obligation to make Laura happy, thus creating an unending cycle of unhealthy codependency.

The causes of personality disorders are varied. There are typically a combination of physiological and environmental influences that shape people. Some studies have traced APD back to specific gene mutations while other studies point to negative experiences early in life. Chris didn't go into detail or theorize how this evolved for Laura, but he was happy they both sought counseling to help each other in their respective futures.

Divorce your Wife; Divorce your Life

The divorce proceedings were finalized. Although Chris had been living away from Laura for several months, it was officially over from a legal perspective. But what about socially?

Now ex-wife Laura, at the courthouse came up to Chris and asked, "Can we still be friends?"

Chris replied, "If you can tell me one person that's treated me the way you've treated me, I'll be your friend" That was it. Chris never saw Laura again.

A funny thing happens when you get divorced, according to Chris. During your marriage you accumulate mutual friends. At first, you think these friends will continue to stand on the border that once joined you and your loved one (now ex-loved one). However, it isn't that simple. As Chris learned, the "mutual" friends from his marriage now turned into mutual spies.

Chris' friends thought it was important to tell Chris about what Laura was doing, who she was with, where she was going. The legal part of the divorce was final, but the emotional part of the divorce continued to wear on like a dusty, meandering, uphill path in the woods with no exit or end in sight. Chris realized he was on this path for almost two years in Melbourne FL before deciding it was time to make a move in another positive direction.

One day at work, one of Chris' coworkers approached him and asked if it would be okay if he started dating Laura. Chris told him, "I wouldn't wish her upon my worst enemy."

It was time for a fresh start. Chris quit his job and moved 3 hours south to Miami. The only way to get emotionally disconnected from

Laura, was to divorce his friends and make new ones.

Chris learned many valuable lessons on this journey:

1. Take action to make your situation better, or it will only get worse
2. Sever ties with people that are emotionally draining
3. Be willing to embrace change

Before moving, Chris' counselor gave him a diagnosis that changed his life:

"You know you're bi-polar, right?"

Episode 4: Benefits of Being Bipolar

Breaking News

Upon learning news like this who do you think he called? Of course, his mom. Mom didn't take the news well, she immediately started crying. Chris needed support. He felt crippled because along with a better understanding of his condition, he also learned a contributing factor was his natural reliance on codependency. Chris wasn't on speaking terms with his siblings at the time...it was a lot to process, so the easiest thing for him to do was withdraw.

Realizing how he emotionally hurt mom with the news, Chris went into a depression. He completely lost his motivation. Now instead of one family member needing support, at least Chris and his mom were both hurting. He had a tremendous sense of guilt for sharing this with his mother, but realized that the only way he was going to get help for his condition was to start talking about it.

Unfortunately, people with Bipolar Disorder can become depressed during their low periods. Withdrawal is sometimes the first reaction, people want to be left alone and not talk to anyone. But isolation can increase sadness, especially those with Bipolar Disorder.

People that are bipolar tend to be more creative. Chris expresses himself artistically and socially in the form of logos. Logos to raise social and political awareness, logos to poke fun of mainstream norms and logos to put smiles on people's faces with his cleverness. Creative expression helps bring Chris peace today, but it wasn't always that easy.

According to a study conducted by Lancaster University, participants with bipolar disorder reported having sharper senses, focus, clarity of thought and increased productivity. While some in the study would like the disorder to go away, many participants admitted they would prefer to keep their condition intact. Some in the study went so far as to describe their experience with the disorder as one of "God's Blessings."

Rebound Relationship

"I am not what happened to me, I am what I choose to become."
~ Carl Gustav Jung

After divorcing his first wife Laura and moving to Miami, Chris spent more time rollerblading and building up his calf muscle. When he was a child playing ice hockey, an opponent tripped and cut his calf deeply. He never felt like it healed correctly. He figured the best way to strengthen the muscle was to skate. Miami Beach was a beautiful place to rollerblade.

While rollerblading you get to take in the sights at your own pace while getting exercise. Of course, you're never alone.

These days, along Miami beach, you still see lots of activity: rollerbladers, traditional four-wheel roller skaters, Segways, bicycles, trikes, scooters, skateboarders, and of course, pedestrians. Review sites like www.yelp.com and www.tripadvisor.com even list the top places to rollerblade while visiting the beach in Miami, FL.

One day while Chris was rollerblading his usual route, he decided to stop at a local bodega. Bodega's are small grocery stores, usually located in Spanish-speaking neighborhoods. Since Miami has such an influx of people from Cuba and South America, it's common to overhear conversations in Spanish. According to an article published by NBC in 2014, the Latino population in Miami was 70 percent.[26] Chris stopped in to buy an apple every day at the little bodega on Washington Avenue. That's where he met Sandra.

Over time, Chris got to know Sandra where he learned that she was a swimmer on the Columbian National Team, similar to being on an Olympic Team from a sports perspective. She lived two buildings down from where Chris' sister lived on Collins Avenue. He spent many mornings visiting her at the bodega and many evenings sitting on the beach talking to Sandra and listening to both the surf and Sandra. Like many people who are trying to make a better life for themselves in the United States, Sandra was struggling.

Chris and Sandra moved in together a few months after meeting. They were making a new life together, but Chris always sensed something from Sandra's past was keeping her from fully engaging in their relationship. He thought that maybe she wanted a commitment, and Chris was in love. Before Chris could finish asking Sandra to marry him, she said "yes!" Chris decided the perfect date to marry Sandra, February 29, 2000. He told her, "You're one in a million, and it will be a million days until leap year shows up in the millennia." Chris joked saying that if they were still together his fifth anniversary was this year.

One evening the phone rang and Sandra's brother was on the other end of the phone. Sandra finished talking to her brother, then coldly handed the phone to Chris. All of the emotion had left Sandra's eyes. He could see by the look on Sandra's face that she was upset. Sandra's brother was talking so fast that Chris couldn't understand what he was saying. After hanging up the phone, Chris finds Sandra in the bedroom on her knees crying. Chris reaches down to hold Sandra's hands, trying to console her, but all she did was scream. While she is screaming, she pulls on Chris' hands, which causes Chris to lose his footing and he falls, burying his knee in the floor, letting out a loud BANG!

Chris hit the floor with such force that the lamp next to the bed tumbled over sideways. Five minutes later there is a loud knock on the door. Chris opens the door and sees two angry police officers. It appears that Chris' neighbor, probably the one downstairs, had called the police.

Sandra comes out of the bedroom and is completely hysterical. She's muttering something in Spanish, and neither Chris nor the police understand what she is saying between tears. In Florida at the time, when the police were called for a domestic disturbance, someone usually goes to jail and that someone was usually the man.

Chris quickly finds his nostrils were filled with the blue coral shag carpet throw rug in their living room. His hands were being clasped behind his back, then he was hoisted and escorted down the steps and into the back of the police cruiser. Chris tried to explain what happened, and all the police kept bantering back with in response is, "We learned all we needed to know from your downstairs neighbor, now shut up!"

After being processed down at the local jail, Chris finds himself on the third floor of Dade County Jail in Miami. It's a dank, humid atmosphere with rain leaking into the room due to the passing storm. After the rain stopped, Chris was ordered to hit the showers. There were no towels. The only thing inmates had to dry off with were moving blankets. An old man had given Chris advice before showering, he said, "Don't dry off with these blankets. After the shower, wrap yourself in the blanket, it will take the moisture off and the blanket will get the smell off your body, because the soap here sucks!"

Chris gets released a few days later because Sandra filed no charges. After he got home, Chris saw that Sandra and all of her belongings were gone. He goes to the computer and it has been wiped clean. Everything ever downloaded was gone and all the browser history, deleted. Chris needs to talk to someone, so he decides to go to a friend's place in Cocoa Beach.

Cocoa Beach is one of the better beaches in Florida for surfers. There are usually steady breakers, but most tourists come to visit Cape Canaveral Air Force Base and to watch Space Shuttle launches. Chris' friend Davey was an avid surfer. After talking to Chris, he offered to have him come for a few days to talk and get his head together. Chris didn't realize Davey had another addiction, online porn.

Chris sent a couple emails to Sandra and the two agreed they would talk between 1:00 pm and 2:00 pm the next day. Davey left to catch some breakers and Chris stayed waiting for Sandra's call. Around 1:30 pm, Chris started to get worried because the phone didn't ring. Back in those days most homes had one phone line. It was either being used to talk on the phone, or as an internet connection. Wi-Fi did not exist as it does today. At 4:00 pm Davey returned. Chris didn't realize that before Davey left, he was downloading porn the entire time. In the 2000's, person-to-person or "P2P" online file sharing websites were popping up everywhere. The surge in file sharing coincided with the invention and release of the "MP3", a digital music file that became very portable, very fast. Napster was probably the most popular sharing site, known for sharing large numbers of files at once. Along with music, scores of other files for sharing emerged, including documents, books, and computer programs. Large files being transferred from peer-to-peer would tie up people's phone lines for hours as digital content was being downloaded.

Three days before Valentine's Day in 2001, Chris was visiting some friends in San Antonio, and he learned that Sandra was working at a Mexican restaurant by the airport in Miami. Chris was able to check in with his contacts from time-to-time and learn how she was doing. The next time he reached out to his friend in Miami to check in on her, he learned she had quit her job and disappeared again.

Chris kept checking his email periodically until 2005. He would send an email once every two weeks to check and see if he could open a line of communication. Chris stopped sending emails in 2005 after realizing he was driving himself up a wall.

In 2006, supposedly she emailed and said she wanted to get back together, but Chris had stopped checking his emails. It wasn't until years later he found the email, unopened in his inbox.

In June of 2007, Sandra filed for divorce in Miami Dade County.

To this day, Sandra pops up into Chris' life every so often. He may never understand why she left or what that phone call from her brother meant. His only theory is that something happened in her past that scared her enough to flee from Florida and disconnect from her ties in Miami.

Musical Reference

Bipolar disorder was once referred to as "manic depression", popularized by the famous Jimi Hendrix song. A few stanzas from Hendrix's poetry put to music sum up bipolar depression very well in the band's debut album, touted as one of the greatest debuts in the history of rock music:

> **Manic depression is searching my soul**
> **Manic depression has captured my soul**
> **Manic depression is a frustrating mess**

> ~ Hendrix, J (1967), Manic Depression,
> Performed by Jimi Hendrix Experience, on *Are You Experienced* [Vinyl]

Chris was clinically diagnosed with Cyclothymia, which is a much less severe form of bipolar disorder. Cyclothymia, like bipolar disorder is characterized by episodes of mood elevation and depressive symptoms over a period of at least two years. We all have a "baseline" of mood as humans.[27] We know when we are in a certain "mood" just as we recognize the moods of people we are frequently in contact with because we know their "baseline". In Chris' case, his moods are more extreme, but completely controllable with counseling, learned coping skills and sometimes medication.

For his entire life, Chris was trying to please people that didn't reciprocate, which complicated and in some cases endangered his wellbeing. Ex-wife Laura created an unhealthy codependency. Regardless of Chris' actions, he could do nothing to make Laura happy. His Mom is loving and caring as any mom, but had her issues raising four children with an alcoholic husband, Chris' father. He believes he learned his codependent tendencies from observing the relationship between his mom and dad. Several close interpersonal relationships in his life developed his tendency to fall into codependent relationships .

Chris' doctor immediately put him on Lithium to cope with the reality of being bipolar. This was before other therapists and clinicians in his future realized Chris' condition was much less severe than many. Unfortunately, this had its own side effects that were sometimes more troublesome than dealing with being bipolar. After all, Chris had been bipolar his whole life without being medicated, but he thought it would be worth a shot.

Lithium really messed with Chris' digestive track. Mom had diverticulitis, his grandfather died of intestinal issues, but no one ever really talked about it. Dad died of colon cancer. Chris was clogged up and felt sluggish. He had a really hard time dealing with the cloudiness.

The development of his disorder was much deeper, and the relationship with his now ex-wife was no help. Chris took the news in stride. If anything, the diagnosis helped validate some challenges he had faced previously and in typical style, now that he knew the issue, he could start to manage it effectively.

What's most important to note about Chris and his struggles with being bipolar, is that he doesn't want your sympathy, but he would appreciate your empathy. He doesn't want you to feel sorry for him, but he wants you to understand why he is who he is.

Chris is a compassionate and caring person who sees the best in people and seeks to help others by sharing his knowledge and experience. He will never be "cured", but he wants to be understood. Sometimes Chris communicates using few words, which makes him very understandable, but others may see this as being blunt, or lacking social grace. Chris' greatest strengths are his honesty and loyalty. Although some perceive him as socially awkward, Chris is a great friend to those of us he has invited to be part of his life.

After Chris' Psychotherapist told him he was "bipolar", Chris' immediate reaction was that it may have had something to do with his dad's exposure to "Big Mike", back in the 50's. But was it "Big Mike", or something else? We'll get to that episode later. But for now, we're going to tune into a story of betrayal and how Chris had to work his way back onto his feet.

The key lessons Chris learned through the experiences shared in this chapter:

1. Be resilient, we can adapt to anything thrown our way
2. Life is a roller-coaster, you need to learn to ride the highs, the lows, and hang on no matter what
3. Accept who you are and be the best you can

Episode 5: What Made The Man Mad?

**don't be MAD
at the man
be MAD
at the man
that made the**
MAN MAD
COPYRIGHT 2012 C.B.F.K.

Chris had a pattern of unhealthy relationships in his life. While he was selling car stereos in four cities, he met Rosemary while making a stop in Houston in 1999. Rosemary was different, she treated Chris with respect, she was compassionate, and Rosemary and Chris became friends. For almost three years Chris would visit Rosemary and her family. He attend family gatherings while he was in town and became a regular at family celebrations, including birthday parties, Easter, Christmas Dinner and New Year's celebrations when he moved to Houston.

In 2003 Pete and Frank's sister Rosemary opened a car stereo and tint installation shop in the middle of Southwest Houston. Chris describes it as a thriving Mexican village of businesses, apartments, and hard-working families. If you've visited

Houston in the summertime, you'd understand why window tinting is a must have.

Since Chris was still peddling car stereos and living out of a local motel, Rosemary offered to have Chris live in the back room of her tint shop. Chris didn't have many things at the time since most of his belongings were stored at the local U-Haul. His friend German had a trailer, so Chris could go to U-Haul anytime to pick up his things when the time was right. The day Chris was moving out of the hotel he was staying at, the owner was mad because Chris wasn't keeping up with payments. Chris got an earful from the manager and promised he would have a payment next week.

Rosemary's cousin German was a good friend. He and Chris were both drifters. Since German was going to help Chris move his belongings out of U-Haul Storage with his trailer, Chris wanted to reciprocate. After visiting U-Haul for a few things Chris started figuring out what he was going to move into Rosemary's extra room. His plan was to get up early the next morning to make at least $300 peddling radios to the local construction workers. This would help Chris settle his tab at the motel and allow him and German to have a place to stay the next few nights while they moved into the extra room in Rosemary's tint shop.

German was busy that evening, so Rosemary's brother Frank and his friend Pete drove Chris to U-Haul to pick up some of his belongings. Chris was supposed to start moving into Rosemary's spare room the next day. The wheels were turning in Chris' head. It seemed like a perfect match. Since tinting and peddling radios both required cars, Chris felt he could earn a decent living learning the tinting trade while upselling Rosemary's clients on new car stereo equipment.

In exchange for Rosemary's hospitality, Chris would help out when needed, including watching her kids. Chris wasn't a drinker, so watching the children became an important responsibility. While the family was drinking and carrying on playing dominoes, Chris was often left with the responsibility of overseeing the kids. Frank reminded Chris of his dad Francis, who would start drinking beer after his morning coffee. In a way, watching Rosemary's kids reminded Chris of the latter years of his childhood while watching his siblings by the pool. Chris enjoyed helping others and making the kids laugh at his silly jokes.

Betrayal

Frank and Chris were walking together on their way to Chris' storage unit at U-Haul. Rosemary's kids were trailing behind a short distance, playing tag on the grass. Chris was about to ask Frank a question...the last words he recalls uttering were "Frank, what are you..." then thwap!!! A closed fist surprisingly landed squarely on Chris' left temple, and he started receiving the beating of his life. The first punch was just pure shock, but Chris didn't go down yet.

Pete, Frank and a third friend jumped in, beating Chris to the ground. All Chris could think of was his first and last conversation with God about what he should do with his belongings at U-Haul. Dumbfounded, Chris could not understand why his friend Frank just sucker-punched him; then Frank's two friends jumped in and were kicking and punching him from all sides while he lay confused and helpless on the ground.

It gets worse…

Chris landed in a pile of Fire ants. If you live up north, you have ants that are red in color, but they aren't Fire ants. In the south, Fire ants bite; they inject a venom that grows into an itchy blister that resembles a white-head pimple. The development process of the pustule is different for each person, but usually takes between three and eight days. People that are extremely sensitive to the red ant venom may experience nausea, dizziness, or even death. In The United States, red ant bites kill about a dozen people every year.[28]

Chris could have damaged any one of them, but he didn't fight back. How could he? Although it was three against one, Frank was his friend and Rosemary's brother. So between thinking about what he was going to do about U-Haul, he figured the best strategy was to lay motionless until the beating stopped...which it eventually did.

Out of his good eye, now throbbing and swelling from being kicked in the face, Chris could see that Rosemary and Frank's wife grabbed the kids while he was repeatedly woken to consciousness being bitten all over his back as he lay in a pile of red ants. Chris was extremely confused and hurting.

Frank hurried away, but he kept looking back. Although Chris was unable to speak, he mouthed the words, "I'm going to kill you", and he knew that Frank read his lips by the expression on his face.

Safe for the Night

The evening of the beating, Chris was in no shape to peddle stereo equipment. As much as he wanted revenge, he realized that would get him nowhere. Chris knew about his urges because of his condition and was now showing that although he was triggered after the beating, he was in control of his emotions and the behavior that got him in trouble as a schoolboy.

Chris could barely lift anything without his ribs reminding him they were broken. Chris sought refuge on the floor of his friend German's mobile home. It didn't have electricity or running water, but it was a place to stay for the night.

German took one look at Chris and with a concerned look, asked him what happened. Chris told German that when he went to U-Haul, Frank and two of his friends jumped him and beat him to the ground. Unusual for Chris, but he ran out of words...all he wanted most in that moment was a safe place to rest. Chris had German wake him up as soon as the sky started to get light. It took Chris almost an hour to get up off the floor of the mobile home.

The next day after the beating, Chris went to Frank and Pete's mother's house, where Pete lived. Chris frequently visited this home where he once felt welcome, but now he felt the need to plan. Chris visited with Pete's mother, where he did not get any sympathy. However, Chris counted the steps from the front door to Pete's bedroom. In a way, Chris was plotting his revenge, but realized it would be better to use this information as a threat than to actually follow-through on any physical revenge. Chris felt psychological revenge would be stronger and more lasting.

Chris realized that since it took him an hour to get off the floor he thought Frank would come to finish him off in his weakened state. After telling Frank and Pete's mom everything that happened the day before and her lack of reaction, Chris felt even less safe. It's almost like the whole family knew what and why it had happened, but Chris was the only one that wasn't told. That next night, Chris decided not to go back to German's house because if Frank knew where he was staying, he would probably try to finish what he started.

Chris later learned that Frank did prison time after getting caught setting someone's car on fire in Southwest Houston. Pete, Frank's brother, did time as well, but Chris was unclear of the charge. If Chris only knew of Frank's mean streak, he would have stayed 10 feet away.

Reflecting back on the beating, there is nothing Chris can recall as to why Frank would have organized and executed the attack. Maybe he was jealous? Maybe he didn't like Chris being responsible and helping take care of the kids? Did Rosemary say something? He will never know. Right now, Chris had to focus on getting well.

Chris found Frank the next morning in his usual spot, sitting in his front yard at 6am drinking a beer. His first thought was to stomp on the gas and feel Frank squirm under the tires of his Ford Taurus, maybe even get caught under the drivetrain and drag him around the neighborhood for a bit before swerving left and right to throw Frank's bleeding body free. Although this impulsive and irrational imagery was attractive at the time, Chris realized this would not help his situation. He still needed Rosemary to help with U-Haul, and while running over Frank would provide instant gratification, it would only land Chris in more trouble and likely in prison. Chris slowly drove by the front yard and told Frank, "I can find you anytime", then kept driving.

Chris kept driving around to stay awake. His greatest concern was that he was going to drift into anaphylactic shock as the venom from the ant bites overtook his system, so he had to stay awake, he had to keep moving. At one point, Chris thought he should flash his lights at the Harris County Sheriff car that passed by, but what would he say? Again, his situation was complicated and may not get better by involving the authorities, so he kept moving.

The homeless community in parts of Houston are very tight knit, they look out for each other. Before Chris started making money peddling car stereos, he had spent many nights living out of his vehicle. He would spare what he could to people living on the street and made some friends with his generosity. After word got out that Chris was attacked, several of Chris' homeless brothers volunteered to give Frank a tune-up, but Chris declined their generous offers. Chris believes in karma and knows that Frank will get his someday, if he hasn't already.

Chris had two blackened eyes and bloodshot from the impact of being kicked and punched while on the ground. He sustained two broken ribs plus over 700 ant bites. There wasn't much Chris could do without insurance and there still are no casts for ribs like other broken bones. Chris didn't want to get hooked on pain medication either, so he decided to let time heal his wounds, but what he didn't realize is time only helped slowly fix his physical pain, his emotional pain would start a steady decline.

The incident left Chris with long-term emotional trauma, more commonly referred to as PTSD - Post Traumatic Stress Disorder. The ant bites on Chris' back have never gone away. To this day, when it gets hot (which is most of the year in Houston), the venom from the ant bites start to swell into red welts on Chris' back. Heat and stress trigger the swelling of ant bites to this day, but he is able to ease the pain with Epsom salt baths and a baking soda paste he makes with water.

In 2006 one of Chris' coworkers (we'll call him Diego) at the ice rink where he worked thought it would be funny to quickly raise his arm and pretend to throw a punch at Chris, as quickly as Diego raised his arm to pretend to throw a punch, Chris ducked while spinning and put Diego on his back with a leg sweep. Diego learned that he shouldn't play like this with Chris at work, or anywhere else. Chris is still in recovery due to PTSD from the attack and still deals with minor pain from his ribs every so often when he gets hit in the right spot playing ice hockey.

Obviously, the deal with Rosemary went south, so he wouldn't be moving into her tint shop anymore. He had no possessions, nothing to sell to make money, and no money. He eventually moved into a halfway house, but for now, he was drifting on his own.

Homeless

Chris knew Walmart was a place he could safely park and spend the night. Sam Walton would allow campers and truckers to stay in the parking lots of his stores to bolster their business. The Walmart on 45 in Houston is where Chris ended up staying the night, sleeping in his car. Chris had to use the steering wheel to pull himself upright since his broken ribs and core muscles were seriously bruised, but at least he felt safe and in a place where Frank would not find him.

Church parking lots were also a place of refuge. Chris learned this is where the U.S. Mail Carriers took their naps during the day. Growing up Roman Catholic and spending many years as an Altar Boy, it was easy for Chris to feel the safety of any church parking lot and see it as a place of refuge.

Chris learned to keep a white towel rolled up and under his arm. He would use this technique to help himself into the pools in the motels and hotels. Chris didn't need a room key to access the pools at the time since most pools were outdoors, all he had to do was walk in with the other guests. It was an easy way to get clean, stay cool and escape Houston's steamy heat during the day.

A local truck driver, Mike Ricardo helped take care of Chris. Mike showed Chris how to get into hotels that were closed down or into rooms of motels with high vacancy. As Chris' luck would have it, he followed Mike's instructions and thought he found a quiet place to rest for the night. Maybe 30 minutes into Chris' slumber he heard the tiny bit clicking against the tumblers inside the lock of his door, he had no place to go. The hotel with many vacancies decided the room he had broken into was the one being rented that night to a husband and wife traveling across the country. Chris was caught by the hotel.

Chris did his best to convince the hotel that they owed him a room for disrupting his sleep. But the owner at the time felt otherwise. Chris was given an ultimatum: leave or get arrested, so he chose the former and got into his aging Ford Taurus and started driving.

Chris became friends with a security guard that guarded the retail complex where the giant 99 Store is on Bissonnet Street in Houston. He encouraged Chris to visit the service station so he could call home thinking maybe Chris could get some help. Little did this well-intentioned stranger realize that Chris was over 1600 miles from his mom in Syracuse. Chris called his mother; it was the last time he would hear her voice.

Chris wound up in the parking lot of the Epiphany Episcopal Church, across the street from Houston Fire Station number 68, which was adjacent to McDonalds. Given Chris' rib injuries, the most Chris could eat in one day was one or two McDonalds hamburgers. Any more, and his ribs would start to hurt.

Clerical Error at U-Haul

While Chris was recovering from the beating, he somewhat lost track of time. There was something he had to do at U-Haul, but he couldn't quite remember what. The next time Chris went to U-Haul to enter his storage unit, the lock on his unit was changed and his key didn't fit, so he went to the front office to find out what was going on.

Chris talked to Cindy at the front desk and asked for help. She didn't have to say a word before Chris knew what she was going to say, "I'm sorry Mr. Kelly, but your storage unit was sold at auction two weeks ago." Chris' heart sank. Everything he had held onto and moved with him from Miami was gone.

Rosemary helped pay U-Haul on her credit card. One of the reasons why Chris didn't punch Frank back is because he gave Rosemary cash and had no proof of his U-Haul expenses. The attorney Chris visited wanted $5,600 upfront to represent Chris for U-Haul. Then, he got involved with James Harrington and the TX Civil rights project who said they would represent him using the legal students at University of Texas that volunteer their time.

Transition of Hope

One day Chris woke up in his Ford Taurus at his usual spot in the parking lot of the Epiphany Episcopal Church. He saw a priest walking through the parking lot and got out of his car and thanked him for not calling the police. The priest asked Chris why he had to be sleeping in his car in their parking lot, so Chris shared his story (well...not the WHOLE story! But you get where this is going). Chris was caught trespassing earlier that morning and kicked out of the hotel where he was squatting. The priest shaking his head empathically, handed Chris a $20 bill and explained they had a human services office in a separate building adjacent to the rectory. He told Chris to stop by there at 9:00 am when the office opened and assured him he could get the help he needed.

The church first put Chris in touch with a doctor. Chris believes in karma. If Chris didn't get caught at 4:00 am and kicked out of the hotel where he was staying, he wouldn't have driven around seeking refuge. Chris would have missed his opportunity to get the help he needed. Chris was very thankful for finding the right parking lot and receiving help from the priest.

The doctor at the Church put Chris in touch with Houston MHMRA - Mental Health and Mental Retardation Association of Harris County (now known as "The Harris Center"). The church felt that would be the best starting point given Chris' physical and mental condition. The next day, he had a 9:00 am appointment with Harris County Social Services. In hindsight, Chris realizes he was lucky he got caught in the hotel room, again reminding himself, "everything happens for a reason."

Halfway There

MHMRA was able to get Chris a referral so he could move into a halfway house. There are many subgroups that live in halfway houses. As Chris described what he encountered, there were recovering addicts, ex-convicts and people with mental disorders.

The government uses halfway houses for parolees in transition or people on probation as an alternative to incarceration. Halfway houses were introduced late in the 18th Century in England as a way to care for child criminals. It wasn't until late in 1896 that Maud Ballington Booth, an advocate for prison reform opened the first privately owned halfway house in the United States.[29]

The halfway house where Chris lived spent only $90 a week on groceries to feed 12 people. Chris got paid $10 to drive the chef to the local Fiesta Food Mart. He used the extra money to buy food and subsidize what was being served in the halfway house. Entering a Fiesta, the local grocery store was quite a sight.

Fiesta supermarkets caters to the local Hispanic and South American community, but few others realize they have great produce and meat for fair prices. Along with having an aisle dedicated to Manteca (Spanish word for lard) in all sizes, you can buy cowboy hats and in some stores, clothing for work. Of course, there is also an ample supply of veladoras. The literal translation from Spanish to English is "candle." But the veladoras in Fiesta are prayer candles in decorative glass jars, usually eight inches tall and typically have an image of a religious figure and a prayer. Here in Texas, the prayers are in English and/or Spanish.

While Chris appreciated the extra $10 per week shuttling the halfway house chef to and from the local Fiesta for weekly groceries, he realized he needed additional income. Chris can be quite charming, he isn't shy and can engage anyone in conversation. In order to make some more money Chris wanted to be selling something again, but still wasn't in the best shape.

Chris was still bruised and recovering from his injuries, but he needed more money to survive. After talking to some of his roommates, he learned that he could get paid for giving plasma as a donation. Even though Chris was bruised and living in a halfway house, the donation center turned a blind eye and allowed Chris to donate plasma. This put an additional $45 a week in Chris' pocket.

In retrospect, Chris realized there are many desperate people in the world and sometimes that is negative. Some desperate people get trapped in their situation and don't feel that they have a means to make improvements. While other people that are desperate focus their attention on how to make things better.

Chris was focused on getting money to improve his situation any way he could. As Chris puts it, "Like math, when you put two negatives together, you get a positive, right?" This was the case in the symbiotic relationship between Chris and the donation center. When Chris started donating plasma he weighed 220 pounds. By the last donation, Chris weighed only 172 pounds and looked like a refugee. The donations were part of his weight loss, but the real issue was the quality of the food in the halfway house.

Chris got tired of the food at the halfway house. Feeding 12 people on $90 was impossible. In Chris' opinion, the only food the chef could buy at Fiesta were things that no one else would eat. The last straw was when the chef served turkey necks for dinner one evening. As Chris recalls, "Sure, you can add a turkey neck to a giblet gravy or soup, but eating one whole for dinner? Yuck!" Chris went to bed hungry that night and decided he had to pay a visit to Harris County Social Services to see about getting Food Stamps.

Stamping Out Hunger

The next morning Chris waited for hours to speak to a representative from Harris County social services about his food stamp eligibility. During his inquiry, the first person Chris spoke with told him could not get food stamps. This was an extreme disappointment. After all, Chris had done his homework and it seemed as though he ticked all the necessary boxes for eligibility.

During this situation, Chris used his bipolar disorder to his advantage. He was triggered. Chris is a rule-follower and believes he was wronged because everything he learned from his sources is that he was MORE than eligible. What happened next? As Chris puts it, "I threw a whole helly shit-fit"; then he was able to get food stamps so he could buy canned goods and have cold, but decent food.

The halfway house was an apartment with five people. Two bedrooms, with another room made into a bedroom. The old man in the house was Mr. Earnest. He had a pumpkin smile. As Chris put it, he had one giant tooth on top and no teeth on the bottom. Chris later learned that Mr. Earnest had tuberculosis (TB). Baylor University doctors used to visit him at the apartment regularly because he volunteered to be in some kind of TB study. Mr. Earnest also convinced Baylor University doctors to take some of Chris' blood to learn why Chris never caught TB, although he had been exposed to people with TB more than once.

When the halfway house learned that Chris was getting food stamps, they moved him to another room in the front of the house. The new room did not have kitchen privileges or access to a kitchen, so Chris' meals were straight out of a can. He best describes his meals during these times as "rations". There was no air conditioning in this new room either, coupled with the smoking policy allowed by the administration in the halfway house, this got Chris motivated to get out.

Smoking was allowed in the rooms at the halfway house and Chris couldn't deal with it. Every night, Adrian, the guy who ran the halfway house would come through the rooms to make sure everyone was in their bed, so Chris got woken up many times during the night. Adrian called Chris into the office one day; Adrian asked Chris, "If I put a crack pipe in front of you, would you smoke it?"

Chris thought of yelling, Adrian was just another drug dealer trying to get a parolees high and hooked again. Chris wasn't a parolee, but he said he felt like was treated like one while living in the house. Chris wanted to scream, "Quit hitting me", then kick some furniture around to create a reason to break Adrian's nose. But Chris turned the other cheek and didn't let his anger get the better of him. Chris turned around and walked out of the office. But Chris didn't want to be kicked out of the house. "Temptation is everywhere", Chris thought to himself. He had enough going on in his life and he did not need a chemical dependency to cloud his thinking.

At this point, Chris had spent several years knowing of and living with Bipolar Disorder. The old Chris may have taken a swing at Adrian. Probably even slammed his own face into the corner of the desk to draw enough blood to beat Adrian to a pulp. Instead of just imagining what he wanted to do, the old Chris would probably have just gone on auto-pilot and done what his mind had imagined. His ability to identify his triggers and control his urges to act out physically were well within his control at this point in his life, which is a critical step for anyone living with and managing their bipolar disorder. But something else was bugging Chris and he was like a dog with a bone, he wasn't letting it go.

Chris visited the downtown clinic every day for almost six weeks while living at the halfway house, waiting to see the doctor about his ant bites and ribs. When Chris finally asked when he would see the doctor, he was sent to MRMRA on the Southside of Houston by Mykawa, Houston's Southeast County Jail. Another 3-4 weeks Chris finally saw a doctor. This is not to be confused with the prison in Sugar Land Texas, made famous by the folk song "Midnight Special" by Leadbelly, later made famous by John Fogarty and Creedence Clearwater Revival.[30] During his visit he learned of SEARCH.

SEARCH Homeless Services helps thousands of individuals and families from their current situation into jobs and stable living environments.[31] With the help of SEARCH, Chris was able to get his teeth taken care of free of charge. He hadn't been to a dentist in years. SEARCH also served a hot meal at lunch prepared by a chef. They had washing services, and even provided free tokens for the bus (back when busses in Houston took tokens as payment).

MHMRA was only two blocks away from SEARCH. One doctor at the clinic didn't see regular patients, he was more of an activity director for those in need. MHMRA had counsellors, showed movies, gave you snacks, it was really a place to stay cool during the day and escape as Chris described, "the smoky drug den of a halfway house", where he had to sleep.

Financial Freedom

One day Chris burst into tears while talking to the doctor at the MHMRA clinic. The doctor let Chris know that he was qualified for social security because of his bipolar condition. On the way to visit the doctor, Chris had an electrical fire in his car and barely made his appointment. The electrical harness in the Taurus was smoldering in the parking lot as Chris entered the building to meet with the doctor.

The doctor immediately wanted to send Chris to Harris County Psychiatric Center because he thought Chris was crying uncontrollably. It is possible the doctor thought that after giving Chris good news he would be thankful, appreciative...that would have been an appropriate emotional response. However, some people with bipolar suffer from a different emotional reaction called *Inappropriate Affect*. People with Inappropriate Affect respond in an illogical manner depending on the situation.[32]

Some with the disorder laugh during a sad moment in a movie or laugh while a friend is telling a very serious story. It is understandable why the doctor's immediate reaction was to get Chris the help he needed.

Chris let the doctor know he was not crying because it was uncontrolled, but because he just lost his functioning car to an electrical fire and was overjoyed to hear the news that he was eligible for financial help. While Chris was overjoyed with the news, he really didn't know how to capitalize on what it meant, or how to take the next step. That was fine with Chris because he knew people that were on social security and wanted to learn from a recipient. Chris learned early that if you want the right information, talk to people in the situation.

Chris continued living at the halfway house. Dysfunction was something Chris had become accustomed to in all the places where he had to rest his head up to this point in his life. One of the inhabitants of the halfway house took a liking to Chris, "Old Man Jim", who had been there the longest. Jim told Chris that his social security disability money had finally come in and he could afford to get an apartment on his own. Jim invited Chris on one condition: Chris would spend his food stamp money to buy groceries and Jim would let him live there cheaply, it was a great deal in Chris' opinion. Chris and Jim moved in together immediately. Jim and Chris lived off Jim's apartment and $160 in food stamps every month.

It can take up to two years to get your social security once you apply. Although the doctor at the clinic told Chris he was eligible, he was never instructed on his next step. Fortunately, Old Man Jim took Chris under his wing and helped him fill out all the necessary paperwork. It was only a matter of time before Chris would have his own income and get the help he needed emotionally and financially. Chris appreciated Jim's generosity, but also realized this was another relationship based on codependency.

Eventually, Jim and Chris had a falling out. Jim kicked Chris out, and he was back on the street.

Strike Juan

Chris took advantage of his network and reached out to Juan. The two had met in the same halfway house with Old Man Jim. Juan agreed to take on Chris as a roommate. Juan was the first gay roommate for Chris. The two got along well, but Juan was disappointed that Chris wouldn't share the bed with him, but not only was Chris straight, but Chris couldn't understand how even a gay man would bed with his new roommate: because Juan had AIDS.

The arrangement with Juan only lasted a few months. Chris agreed to put food on the table with his Food Stamps, but Juan complained that Chris wasn't cleaning the house to his specification. Chris has a high desire to please others, and

Juan was another codependent relationship where Chris' desire to help simply enabled Juan's bad behavior. So Chris, enabling Juan's dictatorship, decided he would take extra special care in cleaning the bathroom and tub.

The day after Chris cleaned the bathroom Juan slipped in the tub while taking a shower and hurt his elbow where the tile wall met the shelf of the bathtub. Jaun verbally assaulted Chris, complaining that the tub was too clean; accusing Chris of making him get hurt. Although Juan could not coerce Chris into a physical relationship, he had masterfully trapped Chris in a negative emotional bond. Chris woke up and realized that he has found himself emotionally connected to Juan, in another codependent relationship with someone that would never be pleased. It was time to get help and get out.

Michelle Gonzales was Harris County social worker assigned to Chris. It was the highlight of Chris' week because she always made him feel welcome. Chris would meet people in the waiting room and learn from them, because they had learned to work the system.

Chris learned that Harris County would pay your utility bill for one month. So the trick he learned from the long-term welfare and social security recipients: they would bring their highest bill within the last few months to get reimbursed. It didn't matter which one, as long as the date was in the last three months. Then, the recipient would use the money to go shopping, spend the weekend in Galveston or to buy bus tickets to visit their relatives in other cities. Once again, Chris learned the best teachers are the people benefiting from the system.

Chris would avoid Juan by walking downtown at the Medical Center. They had a good breakfast at Memorial Hermann. Every Friday there was a huge spread for the homeless. There were plenty of eggs, pancakes, ham and bacon. Chris would eat enough calories to survive until Monday. It would take some time before Chris could be placed in another halfway house.

Food was hard to come by on the weekends for the homeless population because Houston is a commuter city. Canning outside of local business, near street corners, or places where foot traffic would be seen just wasn't the same as the busy weekdays. Occasionally, Chris would visit Fishes and Loaves for meals, but as Chris describes, "There were some scary people down there", so Chris tended to visit places where he felt safe. There was one Roman Catholic Church north of the city that had a lunch for homeless people, but they were always very busy and it was a long journey for Chris to get there and back by bus.

Chris had to leave Juan, he could not take the bickering and daily micro aggressions, so he moved into another halfway house on Cavalcade with the help of Michelle. Cavalcade was several steps down and sideways from where Chris had been before. Chris recalls, "It was home to several rapists, child molesters and serious offenders that had been on parole." Most of these ex-convicts could not get into other halfway houses because of the severity of their crimes. Chris didn't have much choice in the matter because no one wants to leave what he called the "better" halfway houses.

The halfway house on Cavalcade was dangerous. Chris' roommate was a felon. He may have served his time, but he was still a criminal in Chris' mind. At first Chris thought he was lucky when his ex-con roommate was reassigned to another halfway house, but that night, Chris realized he was missing his hair clippers and utensils. One thing Chris realized while living in the halfway house: you were better off owning and using your own fork, knife and spoon rather than risk catching a communicable disease from one of your housemates.

With so much going on in Chris' life between recovering physically and mentally from the beating at U-Haul and dealing with varying personalities and situations, the counsellors Chris worked with worked hard to adjust his medications. Although Chris didn't go into detail on every medication the doctor's tried, he does recall one that did NOT work well at all.

Medical Help

SEROQUEL is one of the medications Chris was prescribed for his bipolar condition. The generic name is QUETIAPINE. Fortunately, Chris wasn't driving at the time because the wiring harness on the Taurus had not yet been fixed. Instead, he was traveling throughout Houston on the bus because it was convenient and he could get free tokens. Chris recalls SEROQUEL was hazardous to his health. While riding the bus, he would black out. Entire periods of time would be lost. One moment the bus would be full of people; then all of the sudden it would be empty and Chris had no memory of what happened in between.

What Chris learned from this situation is when you have an illness, you need to try different medications until you are well. Then, you need to accept the realities of the medication until you're better. Finally, you need to wean yourself off the medication to learn to manage your behavior without the medication.

The truth is: Doctor's don't know what your condition is, until they have determined what it is not.

Salvation

Chris' social security had come through, it was time for Chris to get his own place and away from the hazards he was discovering while living in halfway houses. Chris made it clear that he felt like his life was in danger. The Doctor's secretary, Nikki Amos, had Chris sign a HIPPA release so she and the doctor could talk to Chris' sister Marnie about his condition.

Chris signed over his HIPPA rights to Marnie, because legally, Nikki could not share anything about Chris' medical condition until Chris granted permission in writing. With the formalities out of the way, Nikki and Marnie started working together to get Chris a safer living arrangement than the halfway houses.

Marnie was working at McClean Hospital in Massachusetts. McLean is a psychiatric hospital, and is the largest psychiatric teaching hospital of Harvard Medical School.[33]

Nikki fast tracked Chris so he could get his own apartment, but she also needed Marnie to help get what she needed to fully understand Chris' condition and get him into his own apartment. Fortunately, the doctor that evaluated Chris twice at Ben Taub found no indication of psychosis, which meant he was not a danger to the public or himself.

Chris is grateful for Marnie and Nikki teaming up to help, because he probably got into his apartment much faster than if he had attempted to follow all the steps on his own. The only reason Chris was not on his own earlier is because he was recovering from the beating he took from Frank and his posse. Although Chris had reached another milestone personally by gaining financial independence, a less than desirable milestone soon surfaced.

Mom is Gone

November 9, 2003 Chris' mom passed away; but he didn't hear about it until November 12. It was incredibly upsetting. When Chris finally spoke to his sister about his mom's passing he asked why it took her so long to call? Then he asked, "What did you think she was Jesus and was going to rise on the third day?" The situation was upsetting, which triggered Chris to act out verbally. In retrospect, Chris regrets being abrasive with his sister, it was just how he reacted to his feelings at the time.

Mom's passing inspired Chris to publish a logo appropriate for the situation:

I
HOPE
THIS SHIT
IS OVER
BY
MO_URNING

copyright 2012 c.b.f.k.

On the anniversary of mom's passing, Chris decided the best way to honor her memory would be to spend the day at the courthouse protesting (later in the book you'll learn that it was Chris' mom that inspired him to protest). At this point, Chris realized he was angry that his mom had passed away and angry because of other issues in society, which inspired him to publish another logo:

MAD^e
IN
USA

copyright 2012 c.b.f.k.

Chris' life experiences have led him to learn many things. Some of those experience made him very upset. During one situation with the police, Chris' bike was impounded and linked to a murder investigation. Chris believes this was done intentionally to make it more difficult for Chris to get his bicycle back. At the time, his bicycle was his only working mode of transportation. What Chris learned in that situation: just because people have the power to do things, doesn't mean they should take advantage of that power, which inspired this logo:

MAN IS NOT KIND

COPYRIGHT 2012 C.B.F.K.

CANCEL**L**

copyright 2012 c.b.f.k.

ı**TAKE**ASY

copyright 2020 c.b.f.k.

A**TO**MIC N

COPYRIGHT 2014 C.B.F.K.

A WAY WITH

blaME

BRIT ONG

Other logos can be found on Chris' website, at
www.creadeadtivity.com

Chris enjoys expressing himself through words. It helps him translate what he is feeling into something visual. By publishing the words it's almost as if the emotion leaves his system temporarily while his heightened anxiety subsides. Chris' dream is to sell some of his works for worthy causes.

The key lessons Chris learned through the experiences shared in this chapter:

1. Never give up
2. Find your creative outlet
3. Ask for and get help when you need it

Episode 6: Peddlers, Sales and Scuffles

"In the middle of every difficulty lies opportunity."
~ Albert Einstein

The first job Chris had was selling. His Dad was a salesman, so he feels like it's in his blood. Chris made his first sale at 7 years old.

From 1973 to 2016 The Gravina Garden Center was a fixture in the local Syracuse, NY community. Gravina's hired many local hands to keep the business going. Some employees worked in the garden center caring for plants in the back of the house while others worked at the front of the house, in sales. Gravina's even had a landscaping business that helped many high school students earn a decent wage during the summer.

Gravina's was located just down the street from where Chris lived. They focused their energy on helping homeowners beautify their landscape. Chris noticed that nearly everyone at Gravina's was greeted by name, but at 7 years old, he knew he could not compete with them on that same scale, but Chris had other ideas.

A short walk from Gravina's was a large apartment complex. Chris realized that most people in apartments would not be buying a lot of large landscaping packages from the nursery, but he had an idea germinating that would help make him some money. His idea all started with a tiny cactus that was gifted to him by his Grandmother.

Peddling in His Bloodline

The cactus Chris got from Grandma had babies, TONS of babies. Chris made a trip to Gravinas to get starter planting kits so the babies would have a home. After a few weeks, the babies were big and attractive enough for his buyers. His target audience: Apartment dwellers. At the age of 7, Chris realized that people living in an apartment were probably alone and needed company, but couldn't have a pet. He also realized that if they were going to have any kind of plant, they would need one that didn't need much tending: the cactus was an ideal companion.

Chris would load up his blue metal wagon and he would visit the apartment after school, but before dinner. He realized that the best time to get his customers interested was when they were on their way back to their apartment. So a few days a week, Chris would drag his wagon down to the apartment complex to make a few dollars.

In October 2017, Alberici General Contractors purchased the nursery out of bankruptcy court for $293,000, according to Onondaga County Property Tax data. The building contained asbestos, so the contractors had to carefully look at how to remediate the property before another business took its place.[34]

Francis was also in sales, which is where Chris believes he learned most of his skill. It was really the only thing Chris realized he had in common with his father. It was also the only topic his father would openly discuss. Sometimes Chris would even skip school to ride along on sales calls with his dad all day.

Chris' dad represented Mitsubishi, they had a product called "Diamond Tuna" and Francis was responsible for getting that product onto the grocery store shelves at a level that would get his client noticed. Francis liked to brag about what he was doing, he was really passionate about sales, which helped Chris gain the same passion. As Chris observed his dad in action, he realized that to be effective in life and professionally, you needed to be an expert in communication. Not only did Chris' communication skills help him find his second love, it helped him land his first real job.

First Real Sales Job Under His Feet

After Chris divorced his wife and then their friends, he started a new life in Miami. Since he hadn't explored Key West, he thought it would be a good idea to take off for the week and clear his head. While visiting Key West, Chris met Vila. Her first name was actually Gladys, but they both agreed Vila was a much prettier name.

By happenstance, Chris ran into a man that sold carpet for New York Carpet World, at the time, one of the largest flooring distributors in the country (we'll call him Tom). Tom happened to be dating a woman that was the assistant manager's daughter of the apartment complex where Chris lived. Chris and Tom really hit it off, and before he knew it, Tom was inviting Chris to come to the store to sell carpet, so he did.

Chris was a student of sales. Although he had some natural gifts he used as a child, he was always honing his craft by reading books and attending seminars. In 1982 Chris became enamored with the book, "The Art of Selling" by Tom Hopkins. Along with reading the book twice, Chris and his girlfriend at the time also attended seminars on Neuro Linguistic Programming (NLP). NLP is a language of verbal and non-verbal communication, which gives people a strategic advantage while communicating.

The initial sale is critical to stay on top of the game, but upselling is where the real money was made. Prospective buyers would visit the New York Carpet World location where Chris worked and arrive with an idea of getting new carpet installed. By the time couples would leave the store, Chris had asked them a series of questions that helped the prospective buyers turn into satisfied clients of the business. Instead of just installing a new carpet in a room, Chris would be able to help them picture what their homes would look like if they had multiple rooms remodeled at the same time. This included simple wall-to-wall carpeting through an entire re-tiling of their bathrooms.

The only time Chris tried to un-sell someone on a product was as he describes an "artsy" gentleman that insisted on having his entire 3,000 square foot home redecorated (or as Chris puts it, "infected") with purple tile. It wasn't a gentle lavender tile, as Chris put it, "It was a screaming shade of purple that would visually yell at you while entering the foyer of the home." Chris even told the client, "you do realize that when you go to sell this place, you're going to have to either tear out all this tile or put down a new carpet, right?" But the client would not remove his order. That day Chris learned the client is always going to be the client, and his role as a sales professional is to help them make an informed buying decision, even if he didn't agree.

Although sales came easy for Chris, it was the politics of sales that were frustrating. Chris had the third highest average sales out of 1,200 salespeople in the Region for New York Carpet World. But that didn't satisfy management. Management wanted Chris to increase his volume. Obviously, since Chris was such a high earner for the company, if he just increased his volume the company would make more money. Chris refused to approach sales differently than what he was already doing, and his manager backed him up. The next day, Chris learned that his manager had been suspended for three days.

Chris got frustrated and quit for how he was being treated. In retrospect, the relationship management formed with Chris was similar to the codependent relationships of his past. Regardless of how much effort and results Chris demonstrated to please the other party in the codependent relationship, the other party was insatiable, always wanting more of him. Chris realized the only way to escape was to quit, so he did.

Homeless Again

Without a job, Chris couldn't keep the Miami apartment. It would have been easy enough to find another girlfriend and live with her, but that wasn't Chris' style. It wasn't the first time Chris had been homeless, so he had a friend help move all his belongings into storage and started living on the beach.

Chris being a creative person at heart had harnessed his own artistry thanks to his bipolar condition. Chris was no introvert when it came to befriending fellow artists and holding deep conversations about their craft. Chris befriended artist Victor Edward Leong, a sandcastle artist on Miami Beach.

Victor would ride his bike to get to South Beach in Miami and Chris was usually out on his rollerblades. They got to talking one day and Chris learned about Victor's passion for building sandcastles. While Victor had worked out a deal with the owner of The Mango Bar Hotel so he had a place to crash when he was tired, sometimes when Victor came back to the beach his work of art was destroyed. Chris and Victor made a deal. Chris would guard Victor's sandcastles when Victor was not around.

A Man and His Castle

One afternoon Chris was admiring the scenery at South Beach Miami while guarding one of Victor's castles and this huge man from Kentucky wanted to get close to the castle. Chris asked him to please keep his distance. Jokingly, the Kentuckian kept moving closer to the castle, pretending to poke it. Chris told the man he has been asked to keep people away until the artist could come back and finish his work. The gentleman from Kentucky decided to challenge Chris.

The giant Kentuckian told Chris that he wanted to wrestle, and if he won the bout, Chris would need to let him get close to the castle. Chris did not oblige, but his new acquaintance from Kentucky would not leave without engaging. Their voices escalated and a crowd began to form a circle around the two of them. The stranger was right in Chris' face, which didn't trigger Chris, he had his triggers in check. Apparently, the man from Kentucky felt that Chris had disrespected him by not wrestling with him, so he landed a right-cross squarely on Chris' left cheekbone. Chris never threw the first punch after getting his emotions under control, but he always defended himself.

Chris stepped into his target, a straight punch directly through the solar-plexus taking the wind out of his opponent. The first punch buckled the knees of the burly Kentucky man. Chris punched him two more times before his crumpled body hit the ground. Chris picked him up off the ground and threw him over his shoulder; then as he was launching him onto the other side of the seawall (which was a bed of sand), the Kentucky man grabbed Chris' shirt pocket and tore it into a narrow "v" down to his belly button. The man came back a few days later and Chris asked him, "Which of the three punches taught you the lesson?" The Kentucky man didn't say a word and kept walking; Chris never saw him again.

Victor was always worried about something happening to his sandcastles at night, so Chris volunteered to take the night watch and even during the day when Victor had to step away. Although Chris didn't formally work for "The Sentinels of Sand", the organization formed as Victor took on helpers in his craft, Chris was Victor's first sentinel, taking donations to protect the castles and save enough money to make his next move.

Victor used to build his sandcastles above 11th street, but David from Mangoes got him to move his work down to 9th street and suddenly, Mangoes became an artisan hangout, first inspired by Victor's work. Sophie was the bouncer at Mangoes, who was also Chris' friend.

Chris spent many nights on South Beach into the wee hours of the morning. Some mornings were at the Mango were peaceful, but others were not. While at the Mango one early morning Chris and another patron got into a shoving match. Pushing and shoving turned into shouting, then around 2:30 am and a brawl broke out. Sophie grabbed Chris and found him a safe exit before the police arrived and started asking questions. As cited in the Miami "He appeared to be highly agitated as he screamed obscenities and was clenching his fist as he confronted people," said Det. Al Boza, a police spokesman.[35] The angry patron was boxer and actor Mickey Rourke.

Chris was mature enough to realize that being a sandcastle bouncer would not result in a long-term career path. Plus, he longed to get himself back into some kind of sales role. Chris let a few of his contacts know he was looking to get more steady work, and after a few months, he was able to get a name that would lead him on his next adventure.

Unfortunately, Victor Edward Leong (1974-2016) is no longer with us. It is widely believed he succumbed to Shallow Water Blackout, also known as Freediver Blackout. There is an active GoFundMe in his name. The group organizers would like to honor his memory and memorialize his name along the sea wall on 9th Street and Ocean Drive on South Beach. This was the very spot where Victor started building his amazing sandcastles and stayed for so many years while inspiring others. If you would like to donate, please visit the following URL: https://www.gofundme.com/f/v6xsekys.[36]

How Music Made Money

While living on the beach in Miami on Ocean Drive, he was introduced to a man by the name of "DB Cooper." To this day, Chris doesn't know or believe that was his real name, but that's what he called him. Cooper then introduced Chris to Garreth, who had four offices in the United States that would buy radios in bulk, at wholesale prices, and then sell the radios at a premium.

During the next several years, Chris became a traveling salesman between Raleigh, Atlanta, Orlando, and Houston until he finally settled in Houston in 2003.

Chris learned some valuable lessons working with Garreth, but when the company wanted to change its distribution model and instead sell mobile phones, Chris became disenchanted. There was a great deal of profit made in buying wholesale radios and selling them in volume at a retail markup. The problem with mobile phones is that the margins were thinner and most people were buying their phones from the mobile phone provider with a service. Chris estimated the market was too small to make the same money he was making selling car stereo equipment. The clients were different too. According to Chris, the clients he saw were somewhat unsavory, buying phones, which Chris felt posed a great risk and did not align with his moral compass, so he got out.

Chris read an article in the early 2000's saying that the fattest people in the country lived in the south and Midwest. This made Houston an even more attractive target. Houston being the largest city in the Midwest and Southeast put Houston squarely on Chris' map. Chris' knowledge of Houston from selling car stereos, coupled with his passion for herbal teas and remedies made him realize there were probably a great deal of people he could help with his knowledge, so Houston it was.

In 2012, Texas was named "The Fattest City in the United States".[37] Not exactly a reputation the city took a liking to, but as may say, "it is what it is." This inspired Chris to move to Houston and share his knowledge of herbal remedies and possibly open a tea shop.

Let The Games Begin

Chris found himself in a familiar situation upon moving to Houston: no job, no income. The itch in Chris' mind was there: what can I do to pay a bill? And the answer to scratch that itch: radios. With Chris working on his own, he didn't have any middle-man, no other boss, he knew the system and he knew he could be his own boss. But where would he get the radios? He wasn't going to bother with DB Cooper again, Chris was happy saying goodbye to some of the characters he worked previously.

Chris started by combing through local flea markets to get good deals; then resell the radios. However, some of the radios and car stereos were used and in questionable condition. One man Chris worked with selling radios was known as "El Nino Diablo", or "The Devil's Child." He would tell his customers that as long as you can see his license plate, you have a warranty. Chris knew better than this, all he needed was the right distributor because he knew that ALL new radios come with a warranty.

Chris found a company called Seven Elephants based in California, they made major knock-offs of well known, high-end radios. The radios are quality made and rival some of the high-end car stereos that would cost consumers thousands of dollars. Plus, they came with an actual warranty.

Chris was in business to make money, but did not want to have a bad reputation by selling junk that would not last. There were also a few stores in Houston that had the same products, but Chris was careful not to peddle junk. Even though Houston was the country's 4th largest city, it is probably the world's largest town - everyone knows everyone.

The adventure was in finding prospective clients. Chris would go to the most popular supermarket in the area and pick up a bunch of new home guides. The new home guide in each county was like a treasure map for Chris. He would travel to three or four home sites in a day, depending on time, sales and inventory.

Since Chris spoke a little Spanish, the Mexican workers became some of his best clients. New construction sites don't have much police presence because no one lives there yet. Plus, the Mexican migrant worker population was MUCH less likely to call police for fear of deportation. Even though Chris obtained all of his goods legally, the police always assumed he was selling stolen goods because he had a stack of merchandise visible in the trunk of his car.

On occasion, Chris would be harassed by police and would answer their questions and walk away. Chris was about to sell a stereo and super-bass subwoofer when the county sheriff pulled up to ask questions. All Chris said was:

"You didn't see me selling anything, I didn't say I was selling anything...we're done here."

And he drove away.

Sometimes It's Best to Just Drive Away

Chris didn't always drive away, especially when he felt the need to share his opinion of right and wrong. He never got in trouble while selling radios out of his car. However, Chris did manage to get arrested after being tackled by a police officer after making a snide comment directed at a police officer while riding his bicycle. That story is in the next chapter.

The key lessons Chris learned through the experiences shared in this chapter:

1. Be a blessing to others
2. Make money doing something you enjoy
3. Have fun at work

Episode 7: Misdemeanors

MISDEMEANORS MAKE THE MISTER MEANER

COPYRIGHT 2012 TWO U

People with bipolar disorder experience extreme mood swings. Often, prolonged amounts of time elapse between episodes. Unlike people without the disorder, those with bipolar disorder are less likely to maintain control. This condition may cause the victim to act impulsively, thoughts racing through the mind or in Chris' case, aggressively communicate. On more than one occasion, Chris' direct communication style has landed him in trouble with the law. When triggered, he sometimes speaks his what is on his mind before weighing the consequences of his words.

Bicycle Race

Chris has a strong sense of "right and wrong", and sometimes, he has directly communicated his thoughts with local police. He was peddling his bicycle home one night after working at Sharpstown Ice Arena (now called "Bellerive") where he was the night-shift Zamboni driver. On this particular night there was some road construction, so Chris decided to take a different route home.

Bellerive Drive was a busy street. Chris stayed on the sidewalk during his 4-mile journey from the hockey rink to his apartment on Chimney Rock Road, due east of the rink. One day a policeman had his vehicle blocking part of the street and the sidewalk at the same time while he was filling out an accident report. This triggered Chris to speak out because the policeman was violating the rules and blocking his safe path home.

As Chris was peddling by, he yelled over to the cop, "You're on the sidewalk". All the cop had to say was "Thank you", but that's not how this story ends. In Chris' mind, the policeman was violating the law because cars aren't allowed to park in the sidewalk. The situation escalated quickly:

"Shut the fuck up!", the cop yelled back at Chris

Chris replied in kind by yelling "FUCK OFF!", as he continues peddling down the street.

The cop responds with, "This is official police business, keep moving!"

Chris is almost 10 yards past the cop now and yells a final, "FUCK YOOUUU!" and keeps peddling.

Fifty-yards past the officer Chris thinks the exchange is over, but Chris' weekend was just beginning. Chris sees the police cruiser whiz by him and stop in front of his path. So Chris pulls over on the sidewalk and realizes now he's probably in trouble. Chris still remembers the smell of fresh grass on the perfectly manicured lawn of the professional building where he was tackled.

Chris thought he may get a citation, but when he realized the cop was running at him, he realized he was going to get taken down. Chris threw his bike to the side and as he was tackled found himself face-down on the grass. He fondly remembers the smell of fresh cut grass invading his nostrils as he was forcibly tackled into the ground. Chris couldn't help enjoying what he could in the moment as the arresting officer had his forearm wedged behind Chris' right ear as his head was being pressed into the turf.

Chris was put in handcuffs and his bicycle was impounded. He was booked on the charge of "Interfering with Police Business" and spent the weekend in jail. County lock-up provided all the usual toiletries for short and long-term inmates, but Chris decided he was better off not shaving and to this day, carries a beard almost a foot below his chin.

Upon release, Chris had to spend several hours freeing his bicycle. See, this policeman that booked Chris decided to make his life a little more difficult. Chris' bicycle was intentionally logged in as evidence in a homicide, linked to an actual case file being worked by Houston detectives. Chris had to prove the bicycle was his.

Few people realize this, but in the city of Houston, all bicycle owners are supposed to register their bike to be legal. Chris knew this and even had a registration sticker on his bicycle to prove it. So after the initial discussion with the clerk at the City of Houston's Impound yard, Chris was able to get his bicycle and head home.

Chris knows it's hard to refrain from impulse, especially verbally. So when faced with similar situations today, Chris instead pays a compliment to diffuse situations where he would normally prefer a more aggressive form of communication. He has rehearsed a few key questions and phrases to help him manage his anxiety and impulsive verbal outbursts.

Knife Arrest

Chris hadn't planned on buying a new knife, but he decided to stop at the 99 Cent store on the way home from visiting his friend Bill. Bill lived at Uplift, one of the halfway houses where Chris used to live. He was about to exit the store when Chris found a knife that seemed very practical, it had a round design in the center with three blades and a carabiner-like clip so he could keep it on his belt loop. The knife was only $3.99, how could he resist? Chris bought the knife and clipped it to his belt loop before peddling back to his place on Chimney Rock.

A few weeks later the annual Martin Luther King parade was taking place in Downtown Houston. Aside from protesting at the local court house, parades were a great way for Chris to get his thoughts in front of an audience. Since the parade hadn't started yet, Chris thought he would stop by one of the parking lots where parade walkers were mustering.   The streets in the downtown area of Houston are nearly ALL one-way, so driving in a car can be confusing and dangerous.

Chris was still living in the halfway house and needed to get out – he thought the parade would be entertaining. He packed up his cardboard sign collection and was on his way. Fortunately, Chris had access to free bus tokens he could get almost anywhere in the city. After the bus dropped Chris off he started walking and stumbled into a large group of military-looking students off a parking lot on Texas Avenue.

The High School ROTC Cadets probably weren't expecting someone like Chris to come give them a free pep-talk. After all, ROTC students must be clean shaven at all times and on parade day, in uniform. So along comes this tall, bearded man with an accordion-like cardboard sign. Some were inquisitive, while others that did not share Chris' point of view were combative and making fun.

Chris is passionate about how the military treated his father, the danger Francis was put in and how exposure to "Big Mike" at Bikini Atoll left him sick. As Chris was talking to the group of students a policeman interjected and demanded Chris leave at once. Chris reminded the officer that he had every right to be where he was and was only warning the students of how the government treated his father. Chris explained that the cadets had a right to know how the government treated its people.

When Chris would not leave, the officer grabbed Chris and threw him up against the police cruiser parked nearby. Chris was spun around and cuffed; then as the policeman was trying to put Chris into his cruiser, Chris manually flipped the door-locking mechanism on the inside frame of the cruiser, rendering it inoperable. Every time the policeman tried to close the door, it would bounce back open because the pins that would normally lock after the door was closed were preventing the door from latching.

Chris could see the policeman was losing his cool with the whole situation and Chris started to giggle out loud...this only made things worse. The officer had to call another patrol car to finish the arrest and bring Chris to the police station.

Psych Eval

After the initial arrest and booking, the police decided to get Chris evaluated. The officer escorted Chris to Ben Taub for a psychological evaluation. Chris wasn't resisting, so he wasn't in handcuffs, plus, his charge must have been minor, because he didn't do anything other than piss off the cop that tried to put him in the back of his cruiser.

"Handcuff Him" is all you heard from the female doctor's voice. The hallway was nearly vacant, except for Chris, the officer escorting him, the doctor and two large orderlies dressed in all white. The two orderlies looked like professional football players and easily weighed 300 pounds each.

Chris was escorted to a steel bench and then handcuffed to a stainless steel horizontal bar behind the bench. "I'm going to give you this shot," the doctor said. Chris, with a concerned look on his face replied, "What's wrong??? Is this the reward I get for being the fastest sperm???" in a loud, inquisitive tone.

As Chris puts it, "...after that, the doctor lost her shit." She started yelling. Chris couldn't remember exactly what she was saying in her tirade, but she was clearly mad. Chris prides himself in being able to push people's buttons, but maybe this wasn't the right button to push as he was handcuffed to the wall and being negatively stared at by two 300 lb football players.

The next thing Chris remembers is the orderlies moving into position. He imagines that like football, there must be a playbook to keep inmates still while doctors administer unwanted injections to uncooperative inmates. It didn't take much for the orderlies to steady Chris, but he wasn't resisting anything. All he could picture is the needle breaking off in his body and making a bad situation worse. After the injection, the last thing Chris remembers is asking the doctor:

> "What...did you bring me down to your
> intellectual level now with that shot??? Does that
> mean now we can have a fair fight???"

The next thing Chris remembers is waking up in his secure room at the hospital. Twelve hours later, Chris was transferred to Harris County Psychiatric Center, which is part of Ben Taub Hospital. The third morning after doctors and interns ran a series of tests, Chris was scheduled to have a meeting with a panel of doctors.

Chris was woken from his sleep, showered, then had breakfast before being escorted to the conference room. Chris was seated at the head of the table which was already occupied by eight doctors of varying nationalities but all wearing their white hospital uniforms. One doctor asked Chris what he said to the doctor before being medicated. Chris didn't respond. He thought to himself, if ONE doctor got offended, imagine how eight doctors would react? So, after 15 minutes of silence, Chris was released.

Chris was told his tests came back negative for psychosis, so the hospital had no reason to hold him any longer. The best he can surmise is that Harris County didn't want to spend twice the money in caring for Chris since he already had a counselor and was in housing, so being institutionalized would only cost the State more money. But what was the charge?

After receiving a copy of the police report, Chris learned that he was charged with a Class A Misdemeanor for owning a Chinese Throwing Star, which were illegal in Harris County. Chris went back to the 99 Cent store to find out who made the knife; then he wrote to and received a letter from the manufacturer confirming it was a knife with three blades and not a Chinese Throwing Star.

This situation could have gone better. But sometimes Chris' condition gets the better of him. During this situation his words only made the situation worse. Looking back Chris realizes that it's not a good idea to taunt anyone while you are detained, and especially when you're handcuffed. His words would land him in bigger trouble next time.

Doin' Time

"I Aint' Seen The Sunshine Since I Don't Know When."

~ Johnny Cash, Folsom Prison Blues

When Chris would get angry, he would write letters. What triggered Chris to start writing a barrage of letters was the situation with U-Haul. His belongings were sold illegally and he had proof. The only thing Chris received from U-Haul of Texas was an apology from the front desk clerk, so he decided to write to the County's Civil Court Judge in charge of such affairs to help him resolve the situation.

Chris hadn't received a response from the Judge after a couple letters, so he decided to visit the courthouse to leave his next letter. Still no response. Chris was getting agitated. He wrote another letter, this time, telling the Judge that he had been able to get past security in the Courthouse with weapons and felt like he should talk to her about that too....still no response.

Chris visited the courthouse again, this time, he left his letter with the desk clerk. There were two women operating the front desk, but it wasn't a particularly busy day. When Chris was summoned to the window to talk to the clerk he left a note for the judge and asked that it be hand-delivered today. In a loud and somewhat agitated voice, Chris told the clerk, "...and you tell that judge that she works for me!!!" Chris went home that night thinking he would certainly receive a response after his

134

antics in the courthouse. But it didn't quite turn out the way Chris had expected.

At 3:00 pm the next day Chris heard a loud knocking on the door. There were two cops wearing shirts that looked familiar. The men were dressed in the same shirts and blue jeans as the sheriff that had escorted Chris to Ben Taub when he was getting evaluated after a previous arrest. As soon as Chris opened the door to ask what they wanted he was pulled out of his apartment by his right forearm and immediately handcuffed.

Chris was just thinking his words got the better of him again and he hoped the arresting officers weren't going to bounce him down the concrete steps of where he was living, but they didn't. The ride to the hearing was quick and it wasn't long before Chris was pleading his case in front of a judge, not the Civil Judge he was trying to contact, but a Criminal Court Judge.

The formal charge, "Verbal Harassment of a Judge" is what was read at the hearing. The judge told Chris he had to report to County Jail the next morning and Chris pleaded to have his arrival time changed to 4:00 pm in the afternoon instead. Curiously, the Judge inquired why and Chris explained that he had a meeting with his MHRMA counselor at noon the next day and he did not want to miss it. He also explained that he wanted some extra time in case his unreliable car broke down again and he did not want to be late. The Judge agreed to change Chris' required arrival time to 4:00 pm given the circumstances, but Chris had an ulterior motive.

Having gone to private Catholic schools while growing up, jail is how Chris imagined life must be like for students in public schools. Of course Chris realized later in life this was not the case. He believes his negative view of public schools was verbally beaten into him by the Catholic community where he grew up. He was taught that the education in a private school was far superior to that of a public education. As Chris got older, he realized both private and public education quality were probably the same, but only the uniforms were different.

County Jail wasn't that bad Chris thought to himself. He wanted a 4:00 pm arrival because he knew he would be on the Evaluation Block at that time, and the Evaluation Block was the coldest wing of the jail. Chris figured it would be best for him to cool off before being transferred to his jail cell, which was sometimes ready to receive its tenant, sometimes not.

Jail wasn't that bad for Chris, the Latino inmates taught Chris street Spanish and slang phrases. They also showed him the best Spanish channels to watch, which usually involved hooting and hollering at the scantily clad women on television. The guards would yell for everyone to shut up when they started getting rowdy and vocal.

Chris had three meals a day and friends. He was regularly playing chess, checkers and cards. The County Jail had better air conditioning than Chris' current living arrangement, plus the showers were always hot. Chris would ask questions regularly of his friends, learning about their family lives and believing while he was on the inside he could save a few souls. This earned him the nickname, "Moses" while on the inside.

Chris' bail was set at $50,000. Unfortunately, as Chris puts it, "In the Lone Star State, you can't be a loan", meaning, you can't take out a loan bail yourself out of jail in the state of Texas, you need to have the cash in your bank account. Otherwise, you need to find someone else with money to bail you out. Normally, the person bailing you out needs cash, or collateral worth at least the same amount as your bail. In most cases, people bailing out their friends using collateral go through a Bail Bondsman and would put their vehicle or home up as collateral. Chris didn't have any friends with that kind of money or collateral.

Chris spent 24 days in jail and believes he did not sleep for 14 of those days. The inmates were rowdy. Chris kept writing notes to the guards asking if he could get his medication. He was finally seen three days later and had to pay $10 for his prescription, it was worth it. But before his prescription was filled he had to see a doctor at Ben Taub for evaluation. It turns out it was the same doctor that injected Chris after he made the comment about being "...the fastest sperm", he was worried.

But this time she was very professional and Chris kept his mouth shut. Once again, the doctor's prognosis is that Chris was not a threat, he just needed his medication to deal with his bipolar condition; then he was sent back to his cell.

Chris' bail was dropped to $5,000. Maybe it was a clerical error? Chris' brother Jon tried to bail out his big brother, but the bail bondsman would not take money from someone who lived out of state. While talking to his incarcerated friends, Chris learned five different ways to make meth and all the Spanish swear words and phrases. But what was more important than anything for Chris was getting out. He found a local attorney that visited an inmate in a neighboring cell. Chris gave the attorney his banking information and was out on bail in a few days.

Chris wanted badly to fight the charge. It wasn't clear to him that there was any wrongdoing. Chris consulted with his sister Marnie and put her in touch with his counselor Nikki. Then, they contacted the attorney that bailed Chris out. Unfortunately, the answers to their questions were all the same, Chris could "fight" the charge, but if he lost, he would end up back in jail for much longer than 24 days.

Anytime a dependent of the state is jailed for over 30 days, the state reserves the right to revoke the dependent's privileges. For Chris, this meant losing his residence. Being homeless again was not an option for Chris, so he accepted the charge,

"Harassment of a Judge", which is part of his criminal record in Texas. Chris started thinking that his best shot of independence would be to get himself in a job that would wear him out and keep him from getting in trouble.

Independence at Last!

Chris was able to start working again at Sharpstown Ice Arena taking care of the ice. Along with social security, he started saving enough money for his next move. Little did he realize, his next move was not far into the future.

Mr. Phillips ran Sharpstown, but was getting older. He owned a number of properties that he was leasing for some passive income, but retirement was getting near. Chris learned Mr. Phillips was going to liquidate some of his real estate, so he let Mr. Phillips know he was very interested in a two bedroom. Mr. Phillips sold his two-bedroom condo to Chris, where he still lives today.

Chris often reflects on his experiences to date and can't help but think that his father's exposure to "Big Mike" and the radiation from nuclear weapons testing had something to do with how he ended up this way.

Accidents are Disruptive

Things were going well for Chris. He had been playing hockey regularly in the ISUSA Hockey League at Memorial City Mall in

Houston, TX every Saturday night for quite some time. Chris wasn't sure he would play hockey ever again after his trip home on April 2, 2017. Chris described what he recalls after opening his eyes after the accident, "I saw a bright white light and thought that was the end of me. I was upside down and saw grass and thought that was weird, then looked up towards my feet and saw a blue ceiling and thought, who the fuck put me in a blue coffin!"

Chris was driving a 1994 GMC van called the "Vandura." The Toyota Camry that ran a red light was driven by a drunk driver. The owner of the car was the girlfriend of the driver. The Camry hit the van with such force that Chris ended up skidding sideways across the intersection and rolled upside down with the vehicle coming to reset on its roof. Here is a picture of the impact from the Camry hitting the driver's side of Chris' van at full speed. Notice the muffler pipe sheared and dangling from the impact.

Upside down, Chris got dropped on his head…BAM! He didn't realize that clicking the seat belt release button would work so quickly. But his leg was still stuck between the steering wheel and the edge of the console under the dashboard. He eventually freed his right leg and crawled his way onto the grass outside through the driver's side window.

Chris remembers waking up in the Emergency Room. The technician had just inserted a tube the size of his thumb through his back and into his lung. While all this is going on, he heard someone behind the doctor say, "You owe $100 copay." Chris recalls the moment, "here I am dying on the table in the ER, I can barely breathe, my last words I gasp out, YOU'VE GOT MY CREDIT CARDS, JUST CHARGE ONE AND LEAVE ME ALONE, I CAN'T BREATHE."

More than a quart of fluid was taken from Chris' lung that night. He had two broken ribs, a collapsed lung and internal bleeding. He was fortunate that he survived the crash and believes that the van provided him the safety he needed and was glad he wasn't driving his old Ford Taurus anymore.

The next morning Chris is getting ready for release, but he had to pick up his prescription from the hospital pharmacy. He was in a lot of pain, but it was only after sitting for several minutes in the waiting area of the pharmacy that it was draftier than usual. Chris looked down and realized his left testicle was hanging out of the crotch of his pants. All he could think at the time is the force of the accident must have caused balls to break a hole in the weak part of the fabric. All Chris could do was giggle and think to himself, "At least you're still with me."

Just when we thought this story was over, two years later Chris received a letter from an attorney. It turns out that the girl who owned the car was suing her boyfriend, the driver of the Camry that drove into the side of Chris' van. Since she didn't have insurance she wanted money to buy a new car. Chris called the attorney and told him that she deserved to lose her car for letting a drunk driver operate her uninsured vehicle. Chris asked what compensation the attorney was willing to provide him given the extent of his injuries, and the attorney hung up the phone.

The key lessons Chris learned through the experiences shared in this chapter:

1. Choose your words, others will judge and react to you based on what you say
2. People with power sometimes abuse it
3. Every day above ground is one less day below ground

Episode 8: Creative Genius

"No great genius has ever existed without some touch of madness."

~Aristotle

Chris' creative side keeps his mind occupied, trying to help himself interpret how he sees the world through artistic expression of signs, logos and poetry. While working on the book, this is the first poetry Chris shared, which explains much of his philosophy on life as an experienced participant and anthropological observer of the human condition.

Chris wrote the following poem on a napkin after witnessing an argument in a bar. The man and woman arguing seemed to have perfected this observed ritual of calm, argue, make up, then calm again. Not that the argument was rehearsed, but it seemed that the two engaged in the argument had done this before.

Rainbow Poem

Just something I wrote years ago and wanted to share with you......

A rainbow appears after a storm being just a refraction of light. It is bound to disappear after a short period of time. We need to wait for another storm to be able to see one again.

Just like a relationship we make it through until a fight, then happiness is found after some pressure is relieved. But then again we chase a storm to find happiness.

We hope that someday we find the Leprechaun with the gold. But remember a rainbow is a refraction, just as images that some people put on or ones we have created for them.

The delusion will give us hope since that is what our heart yearns but we are not magicians nor creators.

When life offers a change we know we will not know what to expect but we should look forward to the journey since we shall see more. Then, and only then will we be able to see one at will.

i hope you enjoy and share with your friends....
chris

Although some relationships end in bars and the people walking in as a couple move on, to Chris' point, what are they seeking? Are they looking for the next argument with the same person? Or is this a pattern of behavior they like to practice with multiple partners?

Chris then realized he wasn't the only person in the world that had dealt with codependency. The main lesson here: If you're in an unhealthy relationship, get out of it, or at least take a moment to observe your situation from outside and admit there is an unhealthy pattern and do something about it.

Philosophy

Chris starts every day with his homemade mantra:

"Today is mine, not my problems."

Much of Chris' philosophy has been inspired by life events, current events and the world around him. Here are some notable logos he has created to express himself:

Be Objective...
I'm Responsible...
Be Invincible...
Love Life...
Everything Possible...

copyright 2012 c.b.f.k.

Many people have heard of "win-win", but few have heard of "win-learn". One of the greatest lessons Chris has learned from years of sales and life experiences is since some situations that are not "win-win" are actually "win-lose". Rather than negatively reflect on life, Chris has injected a clear sense of positivity with this logo:

w I n
o r
LEARN

copyright 2018 c.b.f.k.

Political Stance
"The best politics is right action."
~Ghandi

Political activism started in Chris' life earlier than most. When Chris was 9 there was an old bus garage across the street from his friend's house. The garage was bought by Mr. Henson, and he started storing junk cars there. Chris' mom didn't like the idea of it and neither did their neighbor Mrs. Olanzo. Mom went to every house in the neighborhood and collected signatures to halt the sale of the garage, thinking rats would be drawn to the neighborhood.

Chris went to the hearing with his mom holding a poster. It turned out the hearing was just a formality. The decision to sell the garage to Mr. Henson was a foregone conclusion. The meeting was just a ritual to celebrate a decision that was already made. Chris overheard his mom and the neighbors after the meeting and they believe Mr. Henson got what he wanted because he used to work on police cars. Unfortunately, as much as Chris believes our democratic process is designed to promote fairness, sometimes the system is fixed in favor of those in power, which inspired Chris to create the following logo:

$ELECTED

copyright 2014 c.b.f.k.

Although mom's efforts didn't get the result she wanted, she didn't let this drag her down. Mom chalked up her effort as a loss and left it behind her. Within a few months, mom befriended Mr. Henson and started having him work on the family's cars. It only made sense that since she and the other neighbors lived so close by, they should expect only the best service because if Mr. Henson didn't do a good job, he had a whole neighborhood to contend with. So the harsh initial feelings were put aside.

This was Chris' introduction to protesting and community involvement. He learned that you win some, and you lose some. Regardless of what happens, celebrate; then make the most of the situation.

Gym Class No-Hoedown

One of the highlights of the school week was gym class. Chris always enjoyed physical activity. Every week during 6th grade the kids would have one period where they could play indoors. The gym was the old church for St. James and the makeshift stage was the dais, where the old altar sat. It was a strange setup, but easy to ignore after everyone started playing. Some weeks it was basketball, other weeks, kickball. Every gym class started with a game of tag until the teacher blew the whistle and brought everyone into line.

One week the teacher blew the whistle to gather the students to make her announcement: "This week we're going to learn country line dancing", the teacher shouted with enthusiasm. Chris was mortified. He could see from the looks on the faces of his fellow students, they weren't very bought into the idea of dancing either. Chris wanted to play sports, not dance or spin in a square, circle, or any other shape.

Chris organized a revolt. He started yelling at his classmates, "Does everyone really want to dance????" he shouted emphatically. If you don't want to dance meet me over here and we'll do something fun while everyone else is dancing. Chris was able to muster a decent sized crowd, he estimates that one-third of the class joined him. Nearly all the boys and even a few girls.

The scowl on the teacher's face was most memorable as Chris recalls. The gym teacher blew the whistle and demanded all those that joined the revolt assemble on the stage at once. She threw a kickball to the remaining students and asked them to pick teams and get a game started. Then she disappeared into her office and returned with a stack of paper and pencils.

Angrily stammering, "Here is your assignment for gym class today, you need to write out the lineage of Jesus Christ!" The way she finished her sentence it was practically a curse, but the boys knew they had gone too far when disobeying their teacher. Almost 20 students silently found spots where they could work with their paper and pencil. No desks, just sitting cross-legged on the deteriorating oak flooring where the altar once stood. Chris remembers making no eye contact with any of the other students, just heads-down and completing their assignment.

Few people today would even know where to start to complete such an assignment (aside from looking it up on the internet). The New Testament explains the lineage many have forgotten, but while attending Catholic School, it was common knowledge. It can be found in Matthew 1:2-16 and Luke 3:23-38. Jesus' lineage begins with Abraham and after 41 generations ending in Matthew 1:16, "And Jacob begat Joseph the husband of Mary, of whom was born Jesus, who is called Christ."

Conscientious Objector

In Chris' neighborhood he recalls quite vividly the stop sign at the end of his street, "Stop The War!":

Photo by Ben Mater @benjmater www.unsplash.com

The Vietnam War was not popular with the people in the United States. Veterans of the war wore their jackets with pride, expecting to be welcomed as the heroes of previous generations. Chris could tell that the locals didn't appreciate the Vets, and the Vets carried a chip on their shoulder expecting to be respected, but that was not the case, the Vietnam war was different.

While Chris was in 6th grade watching television one night he saw draft cards being picked live on the news. Chris used to sit there in amazement thinking that people were being randomly picked in a twisted lottery and the winners may be going to Vietnam to die. Chris decided the best thing he could do would be to write a letter to the head of his school and church, Bishop Harrington. Upon completion, Chris delivered his letter in a sealed envelope, stating his position as a "conscientious objector" so he could protect himself and not go to war. Chris handed the letter over to the Bishop's secretary and never heard anything further.

Plowshares Influence

Chris was strongly influenced by the Berrigan Brothers. People better know the brother's "Plowshares Movement", a Christian pacifist movement that was against the creation and proliferation of nuclear weapons. Since Chris' dad fell ill from nuclear fallout, the Plowshares Movement seemed like a fitting cause to follow. They were best known for their symbolic protesting, which often involved damaging military property and weapons.[38]

The Plowshares Movement borrowed its name from the Bible, in the Book of Isaiah

> "And many people shall go and say, Come ye, and let us go up to the mountain of the LORD, to the house of the God of Jacob; and he will teach us of his ways, and we will walk in his paths: for out of Zion shall go forth the law, and the word of the

LORD from Jerusalem. And he shall judge among the nations, and shall rebuke many people: and they shall beat their swords into plowshares, and their spears into pruning hooks: nation shall not lift up sword against nation, neither shall they learn war anymore."

Right Left and Center

Chris prides himself as someone who is in the "middle middle." Some experts refer to this as "centrism", a political viewpoint where its followers believe in a balance of social equality and social hierarchy while at the same time, opposing political changes which would result in a significant shift in society to either the right or left. Chris is socially liberal and fiscally conservative. He doesn't have an affinity for either party in control today, which inspired him to create a logo to express his opinion:

$$REPU_{KE}^{BL}ICAN$$

$$DEMO_{N}^{C}RA_{P}^{T}$$

$$4^{U}R$$

$$DEMON_{H}^{O}C^{R^{A}}Z_{Y}$$

copyright 2012 c.b.f.k.

Here's how to read the logo: Republican puke, Democrat demon rat crap, for your demon, oh, crazy.

154

Some of Chris' political and social viewpoints have been shaped by his upbringing and others during his experience being homeless. He grew up in a middle-class neighborhood where the nuclear family was intact. All of Chris' friends had a mom and a dad and the majority of his neighbors all worshiped at the same Roman Catholic church. Living on the streets as an adult after the divorce with Laura taught Chris a different view of society, including what he had to learn to survive while being incarcerated.

Play Ball!

Chris was never a violent protester. Instead, he channeled his energy by being vocal in public places and courthouses where other people of the same mindset tended to congregate. Chris was trying to "egg on" the crowd and was approached by Homeland Security near the employee's entrance at Minute Maid Park, home of The Houston Astros. It was a big game for the Astros and George Herbert Walker Bush was in attendance. Chris was the only protester to show up. He was shouting to remind people that while "HW" (George Herbert Walker Bush) was in attendance, they should take the opportunity to share their opinion.

While being questioned by Homeland Security, Chris was polite and courteous in answering all their questions. Chris was asked to be quiet and asked by Homeland Security what he had against this country. "Nothing", said Chris. "I have nothing against this country, I'm just encouraging everyone to tell the President what they think...since he's going to be here anyway, it seems like the best time to do it." Homeland Security asked Chris to leave, so he did.

While walking down Crawford street Chris had an idea! Since he couldn't speak his mind, why not put his words on paper? Two blocks into his walk, Chris decided that all he needed was four words to get his point across. "NO MORE BUSH It":

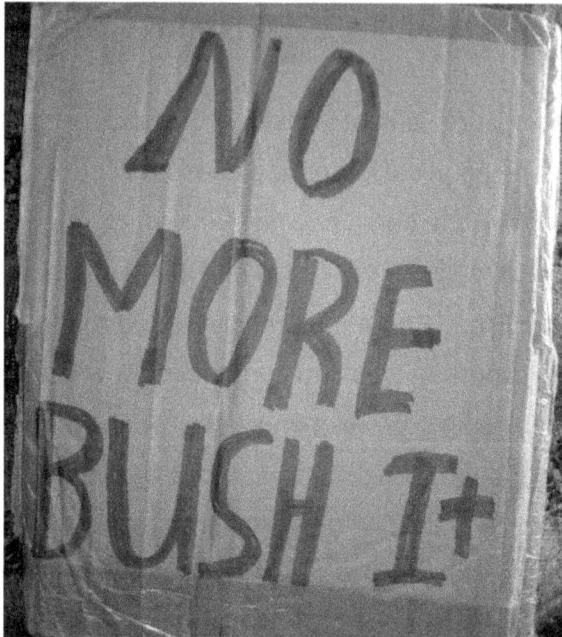

The Houston Police noticed Chris returned to Crawford Street to share his thoughts on the President and received a ticket. Chris' citation was based on an old Houston TX law that most people had probably never heard of before, but it was the system's way of silencing his voice. Meanwhile, hundreds of other Astros fans filing into the stadium had their own signs, "Go Astros" and "We Love the Astros". As promised, Chris wasn't being loud, he was simply carrying his sign, "NO MORE BUSH-IT".

Chris' homemade sign on corrugated cardboard was his way of colorfully making his opinions known and feelings towards the current political establishment. It was also Chris' polite way of being upfront about what was happening currently in life and in the past.

Thousands of Astros fans headed into Minute Maid Park at 501 Crawford St, Houston TX to watch the Astros baseball game during their playoff run on October 8, 2004, so was Chris Kelly. Chris was asked by the media why he chose to pick that venue, to which he replied:

> **"I figured if there was a crowd of people, I could get more people to look at my sign so I figured at the baseball game would be a perfect place to be able to do something like that."[39]**

The sign got the attention of many fans, but also captured the attention of the Houston Police Department. The responding officer tried to take Chris' sign, so he pulled the sign away from the officer's grasp and put his body between his outstretched arms and the officer's reach. This went on for a minute or two before reinforcements arrived.

Five officers responding tried to wrestle Chris and his sign to the ground, but Chris changed his position and was close enough to the employee entrance door to slip his arm through to lock his arm between the handle and the door. It was very difficult for the officers to pull Chris free from the door. At the time, Chris wore carpenter's pants. Unfortunately, one of the officers figured this out and grabbed on to the hammer loop just above the right knee of his pant leg. Chris thought he was going to eat the pavement as he was horizontal with the ground, but with his right arm firmly locked on the door handle with his left hand closing the loop with his wrist, Chris wasn't going anywhere.

Chris looked up and noticed the local news. He noticed the cameras were pointed in his direction with the responding officers so Chris started screaming like a little girl to attract the media's attention. It didn't quite work out the way Chris had hoped...yet.

The Police ended up breaking Chris free of his tiresome hold. He was handcuffed immediately and put into the backseat of a police cruiser. The Houston City Police drove Chris around and eventually dropped him back off where he was detained, but at that point, Chris' audience had all filed into Minute Maid Park to watch the game.

Chris' opportunity to inspire and inform disappeared, just like his First Amendment Rights. The police issued Chris a ticket for an obscurely known and selectively enforced dating back to 1970. The citation was Chris' ticket to help protect The First Amendment. Chris made eye contact with one of the reporters that had seen his struggle with the police earlier and struck up a conversation. The reporter was kind to Chris and empathized with his situation. She agreed it was a violation of his rights. She took Chris' information and later put him in touch with a Civil Rights Attorney.

Fun Fact: The Astrodome

Before the Astros moved across town to its new venue Minute Maid Park, they used to play in the world-famous Astrodome, which was once called "the eighth wonder" of the world. After construction, natural grass was installed as the playing field, but it did not last long after opening on April 9, 1965.[40] The dead grass was then replaced with artificial turf, which became known as "Astro-turf", not just in Houston, but around the world.

Time for Action

Chris felt like his First Amendment Rights were violated, so he did what any red-blooded American would do in the same situation: Sue the government! Chris filed a lawsuit in Federal Court at once to get the ordinance repealed. He also sued the arresting officer and his cohorts that wrestled him off the door.

Chris and his Attorney Randall Kallinen had hoped that Houston's City Council would be able to repeal the ordinance after stating their case. During an interview with the news on the topic, Chris had this to say:

"I think this will open up freedom of speech for everybody in Houston without being prosecuted. I hope this is at least accomplished."

While in Court, the Judge asked Chris for his plea, and Chris replied, "Your officer was silly", and the Judge responded, "I will take that as a not guilty plea and will set a court date to further review the matter."

Chris was aggravated that the matter wasn't dropped right then and told the Judge that he will declare war right here and now to fight for his First Amendment rights and the rights of those that come before this court with the same issue. In that instance the Judge knew this situation was going to get real...the Judge picked up the phone and told the District Attorney to meet in his chambers.

Some time passed when the District Attorney (DA) and Judge returned to the courtroom. The DA read the ticket out loud and let the court know that he couldn't agree more with Chris' arguments. After disappearing for 10 minutes, the DA returned and announced the ticket and charges against Chris had been dropped.

Justice Served

The City of Houston agreed to pay Chris approximately $25,000 for his legal fees and the ticket issued by the Police for carrying the sign was dismissed in court.[41] According to a newspaper article published by The Houston Chronicle, The terms of the settlement also required city attorneys to recommend that the City Council rescind the ordinance banning the carrying of posters without a parade permit.[42]

The key lessons Chris learned through the experiences shared in this chapter:
1. Words mean more when they are in writing
2. Be ready for the consequences of your beliefs
3. Resisting is okay, but violence is unnecessary

Episode 9: Something Else

"What does not kill you makes you stronger"
~ Friedrich Nietzsche, German Philosopher

Chromosome 22 contains hundreds of genes that are programmed for making proteins. Proteins are critical in brain development. Issues with Chris' brain may have been caused by a mutation of the gene. He and his sister Marnie suspected it was Francis' exposure to radiation while being stationed in The Marshall Islands that may have created this issue for Chris and the multiple miscarriages between Chris and his parent's next child.

One of the Genes in Chromosome 22 may cause problems with the development of the brain if it isn't properly sequenced. Specifically, later in life, issues with this chromosome can lead to anxiety disorders and can increase the possibility of other mental health disorders.[43]

Chris was always curious about Francis' exposure to "Ivy Mike" and the long-term effects of the radiation he was exposed to during his service in the Air Force. A recent article in ScienceDaily summarizes a direct link between faulty sperm and miscarriages. Before today, miscarriages were classified as an issue with the woman carrying the child (hence the name), but this recent research published suggests that not only the eggs and uterus, but the sperm dictates the health of a pregnancy. [44] The government would come visit Francis at least once a year to check on him. Dad would never talk about it, but according to Chris, "They were definitely G-men."

Chris believes that his sister Marnie sought a career in helping others because of what she experienced with her father. She earned her Master's Degree in Social Work from Fordham University in New York City and was a Licensed Clinical Social Worker. Chris always felt that he and Marnie had a special connection. She was always there for him. Marnie even moved to Miami to live with Chris after his divorce. Marnie lost her battle with cancer and passed away on October 9, 2013.

Unfortunately, none of Chris' paperwork or diagnoses are available since U-Haul sold his things.

Episode 10: Ice Hockey and Giving Back

"I skate to where the puck is going to be, not to where it has been."

~ Wayne Gretzky

Chris' childhood friend Tim told him on Thursday night they were signing up for hockey on Saturday at the State Fairgrounds. Tim came from a typical Irish Catholic family and had 8 siblings. Chris didn't know much about hockey but knew enough that he wanted to learn to play.

Although the walk to school was short, Friday morning Chris decided to take his time getting ready for school. This meant that his dad would have to drop him off on the way to work and Chris could get the chance to talk to dad without anyone else around.

Chris knew he was Dad's favorite. Unfortunately, this created quite a rivalry among his siblings. Without understanding all the social dynamics of the family, Chris knew enough to realize that getting his dad alone was his best chance of getting what he wanted.

As Chris' dad yelled up the stairs to remind Chris he would be late for school, Chris asked if he could get a ride. Of course, dad said yes. Chris hopped into the front seat of the old Ford LTD Station Wagon with green metallic accent and faux wood paneling. After the car backed down the driveway, there were two loud, but muted clicks as dad shifted the car from reverse, through neutral and into drive. As the car rolled down the street Chris asked his dad if he could sign up to learn to skate on Saturday; by the time the car had traveled past only two houses in the neighborhood, his dad said "yes".

The very next day at The New York State Fairgrounds in Syracuse, Chris and his dad were the third people in line to sign up for hockey. Chris' first experience learning to skate was in a cattle barn that was made into an ice rink. There wasn't a lot of formal coaching for kids that age. The group organizing the skate just wanted kids to get out and be able to practice moving around the ice without falling.

Learning to Skate

Like most kids learning to skate during this time, Chris was given a folding metal chair, the kind you would find at an all you can eat spaghetti dinner in the basement of the Catholic church during a fundraiser. But Chris' chair was distinctly memorable. Best he can tell, it was probably a chair from the weekly Friday night Bingo game where all the old people went to gamble (in the name of fundraising). He knew it was from Bingo because the chair reeked of stale cigarettes.

The smell of the cigarettes blended with the wafting odor of livestock in the crisp air of a Syracuse winter was quite memorable. What was missing from Chris' experience were formal coaches. Chris was wearing a pair of hand-me-down skates, which barely had any support or padding like today's models. The skates didn't tie or fit well, but his passion for learning to skate made it easy to forget what was going on at the time.

After the first year of learning to skate, Chris finally was able to get some equipment and join an actual team. He was having the time of his life. Skating with people he knew from the neighborhood and from school was an exhilarating experience. The next year, at 8 years old, their team won the championship. The year after that at the age of 9, Chris played goalie for his team and defended their championship title.

Chris' family didn't have much money, so fundraising was critical if he was going to continue playing. At 9 years old Chris had to sell $125 worth of raffle tickets to keep playing and to offset the money his parents had to pay out-of-pocket. Chris was determined to sell as much as possible to keep skating. That day, he canvassed the neighborhood and surrounding streets. By noon he had sold $108 worth of raffle tickets. Some of his teammates were unhappy with him because Chris visited their neighborhoods. Sales is a competitive profession, and one that Chris enjoyed. He learned at the age of 9 and then later in life, that while working in sales, sometimes your coworkers will be disappointed in your success.

Chris played travel hockey at Valley Youth Hockey. The nice thing about being in upstate NY is the local towns flooded the pavilions to create ice rinks. In the winter time in Syracuse, you could drive 20 minutes in any direction and find someplace to skate. As Chris recalls, "Sometimes, we would play two games in a day. Binghamton to Oswego NY, from Rome, Utica to Rochester." Chris got to play ice hockey on some of the best ice surfaces in the country, by skating on the rinks of the local colleges.

The year after the team's second championship Chris got hurt while playing goalie. Danny Knowles was skating down the ice and he was the leading scorer of the league. When Chris wasn't in net, he played forward and was the league's 4th leading scorer. Chris' line scored almost every time they were on the ice. Danny took off down the ice and Chris dove out of his crease towards him. As Chris was sliding towards the puck, Danny was in mid-air trying to find a patch of ice for a clean landing, But Danny's skate blade cut through the back of Chris' sock and deep into his calf muscle. There was a pool of blood left on the ice.

Chris laughed about getting his leg cut, but it was more serious he had imagined. The wound probably needed stitches, but in typical Irish Catholic fashion, if you weren't giving birth or dying, you had no reason to go to the hospital. Mom made Chris miss two days of school, which was enough time for the cut to stop bleeding. The muscle Chris' leg never healed right. As Chris got older and realized his weak leg needed help, he took up roller-blading on South Beach in Miami to help rebuild the muscle.

Coaching

Chris' first experience coaching was back in the Valley League where he grew up playing. Mom wanted brother Jon to play hockey. He was too old to play mites, but Mom and Chris were able to convince the league to let him play on one condition: Chris would join the league as a coach. Jon was a small kid so he could pass for the same age group as the Mite-level. Youth hockey in North America is organized into the following labels and age groups:

Age Group	Level
5-6	Mini Mite
7-8	Mite
9-10	Squirt
11-12	Peewee
13-14	Bantam
15-16 / 16u	Minor Midget
15-18 / 18u	Major Midget

Although the groups listed above existed at the time Jon was learning to play hockey, the levels have since been relabeled based only on age starting in 2016.[45]

Chris' main advice for Jon and other children in his early days of coaching he recalls sharing over and over again, "Believe, and you can Achieve", inspired him to come up with this logo:

ACHIEVE
BELIEVE

copyright 2014 c.b.f.k.

Youth Entry-Level Skating School (YESS)

Chris' love for ice hockey never went away. In 2019, Chris was asked to help a group of disabled American Veterans practice sled hockey at The Memorial City Mall in Houston TX. The group of Veterans practiced using half the sheet of ice and participating in a couple tournaments a year.

No coach likes to see ice wasted. So while assisting with the coaching of the sled hockey veterans, Chris was asked to help a couple youngsters learn to skate on occasion. Harkening back to his memories of skating in the cattle barn, Chris wanted to make sure anyone he coached had a structured learning experience.

At first, Chris didn't have enough unskilled players to teach, so his hour of coaching was more of a "stick-and-puck", which is when players take the ice and scrimmage and Chris would offer one-on-one instruction to those who were in need. Over time, enough children and adults, and some with mental or physical disabilities learned of Chris' program. Chris needed help to offer more instruction, so he recruited Jim Molloy as his assistant coach. Together, they began a structured coaching program that followed the USA Hockey Learn-to-Skate Curriculums in Levels 1-3. Chris had up to 12 children in the program at one time with the ultimate goal of the program to prepare skater to compete in local leagues at their age and skill level.

Carl Sasyn was the General Manager of Ice Skate Memorial City and helped Chris to officially get the YESS program off the ground. Learners are not charged a fee. The goal of the program is to have learners "graduate" from YESS and make them eligible to play in the leagues in and around Houston, which have their own cost. Carl's main involvement was to ensure all players were registered, had the right equipment, and were being taught appropriate safety techniques.

Carl's latest venture is all about safety with a new technology killing viruses and bacteria that can potentially compromise our immune system. From athletic equipment to home and offices spaces, Triple O-Zone Technology is available to help. Reach out to Carl at 832-277-4798 for consultation and service:

Carl Sasyn, Director of Operations
Triple O-Zone Technology
6125 West Sam Houston Parkway N. STE 503
Houston, TX 77041
http://tripleozone.com/

This is extremely personal for Chris because he remembers how money was always an issue in his house growing up. Since ice hockey is an expensive sport he volunteers his time to eliminate the cost most families incur during learn-to-skate programs.

While parents of the program continue to try and give Chris and Jim money and/or gifts for their coaching time, the YESS program encourages parents to make regular donations to Texas Sled Hockey. Each tournament costs the sled hockey team approximately $7,600. Donations are tax deductible since www.TexasSledHockey.org is a 501c3 organization. We encourage readers to make a donation if they are so inclined, just visit the web site or scan the QR code below:

Chris enjoys playing hockey Saturday Nights and to this day, imagines his dad standing in the corner of the rink, watching the game while sipping his coffee. Chris earned the nickname "Gandalf", the famous wizard in J.R.R. Tolkien's novels "The Hobbit" and "The Lord of the Rings."

Epilogue: Who Is The Last American Cowboy?

Chris Kelly was born in Syracuse NY on September 28, 1962. Like that of a cowboy, his life's journey is one of an untamed and independent spirit, moving through life. His life story is one filled with challenge, resilience, and self-reliance. Regardless of what he has encountered in life, Chris gets up, dusts himself off and keeps going. Chris does not let life's events define him, he defines himself, and he is not bound by the world's imaginary rules. He enjoys listening to music, especially Bob Marley, which helps him to relax and cope with his PTSD. Instead of writing or yelling at public officials, Chris now expresses himself artistically by creating logos.

His cats Hugo and Zeb (because of his Zebra stripes) hang out with Chris at the condo and take long naps while Chris watches two news channels at the same time. Watching both channels at the same time allows Chris to process both divergent media views to help form his own opinion.

His hope for the readers of this book is to get a glimpse into the life of the many forgotten suffering from mental illness. The media often talks about the world's "1%", the small, elite group our governments rely on so heavily to pay the lion's share in taxes and keep people employed. But there are almost 3% that are completely unknown. Almost 3% of the population are mentally ill, are misunderstood and under-served. Many within the 3% are perfectly capable of being employed and taking care of themselves, but like everyone else, want to be treated fairly.

Lessons Learned

There are many lessons one may learn from reading the entirety of this book. Here are the top lessons Chris has learned as a result of his life's experiences:

1. Racism is stupid
2. Speak up for what is right and what you believe in
3. Think before you speak or act
4. Don't dwell in bad relationships, get out!
5. Take action to make your situation better
6. Embrace change
7. Life is a roller-coaster, learn to ride the highs and lows and hang on no matter what!
8. Love who you are
9. Find your creative outlet
10. Ask for and get help when you need it
11. Be a blessing to others
12. Make money doing something you enjoy
13. Have fun at work
14. Choose your words, others will judge and react to you based on what you say
15. Every day above ground is one less day below ground
16. Words mean more when they are in writing
17. Be ready for the consequences of your beliefs
18. Resisting is okay, but violence is unnecessary
19. Adjust to new reality
20. Seek treatment if you're not well, and keep adjusting the medication until you feel right
21. Exercise is critical for a healthy mind, body and spirit

So the next time you encounter someone that's different, consider they may be part of the 3%. Maybe they don't talk the same, maybe they look different, maybe they blink more often, or not at all. Please take the time to treat these people as you would like to be treated. Ask them questions, have a conversation, take the time to find out who they really are, and you'll be pleasantly surprised. After all, we are all part of the same group, The Human Race.

End Notes

[1] Celebrities with Bipolar Disorder https://www.webmd.com/bipolar-disorder/ss/slideshow-celebrities-bipolar-disorder

[2] Bipolar Disorder (manic-depressive illness) https://mentalillnesspolicy.org/medical/bipolar-facts.html

[3] Our Impact: By the Numbers https://www.treatmentadvocacycenter.org/evidence-and-research/fast-facts

[4] Sex Abuse and The Foster Care System https://www.focusforhealth.org/sex-abuse-and-the-foster-care-system/

[5] 6 Quick Statistics on the Current State of Foster Care https://www.ifoster.org/6-quick-statistics-on-the-current-state-of-foster-care/

[6] Gladeck, F. R.; Hallowell, J. H.; Martin, E. J.; McMullan, F. W.; Miller, R. H.; Pozega, R.; Rogers, W. E.; Rowland, R. H.; Shelton, C. F.; Berkhouse, L.; Davis, S.; Doyle, M. K.; Jones, C. B. (1982). *Operation IVY: 1952* (PDF). Defense Nuclear Agency United States of America. p. 2. https://en.wikipedia.org/wiki/Ivy_Mike#cite_note-Gladeck-17

[7] Vintage photos show the devastating impact of the largest ever nuclear tests conducted by the US https://www.insider.com/photos-the-largest-ever-nuclear-tests-conducted-by-the-us-2019-10#the-largest-of-the-tests-exploded-over-bikini-atoll-on-march-1-1954-it-was-a-15-megaton-explosion-called-castle-bravo-1000-times-more-powerful-than-the-bomb-the-us-dropped-on-hiroshima-in-1945-10

[8] Wikipedia, the free encyclopedia Bikini Name History https://en.wikipedia.org/wiki/Bikini

[9] The Le Moyne College Green Book (2011), Office of Mission and Identity, p. 13 https://echo.lemoyne.edu/Portals/0/Le%20Moyne%20Green%20Book.pdf

[10] Hinrichs J, Defife J, Westen D. Personality subtypes in adolescent and adult children of alcoholics: a two-part study. J Nerv Ment Dis. 2011;199(7):487-98. doi:10.1097/NMD.0b013e3182214268

[11] How Sniffing Glue Affects Your Health https://www.healthline.com/health/sniffing-glue#glue--sniffers-high

[12] Wikipedia, the free encyclopedia https://en.wikipedia.org/wiki/Francis_James_Harrison

[13] Wikipedia, the free encyclopedia https://en.wikipedia.org/wiki/President_of_the_University_of_Notre_Dame

[14] The NYC blackout of 1977 happened 42 years ago today https://ny.curbed.com/2019/7/13/20693407/new-york-blackout-1977-power-outage-history

[15] Wikipedia, the free encyclopedia https://en.wikipedia.org/wiki/Rudy_Ruettiger

[16] A rectory is a residence housing clergy; are used by Catholic and other denominations.

[17] Wikipedia, the free encyclopedia https://en.wikipedia.org/wiki/Ronnie_James_Dio

[18] Wikipedia, the free encyclopedia https://en.wikipedia.org/wiki/The_Post-Standard

[19] Wikipedia, the free encyclopedia https://www.britannica.com/topic/Newhouse-family

[20] Bipolar Disorder: Struggling with Aggression https://www.recoveryranch.com/addiction-blog/bipolar-disorder-struggling-with-aggression/

[21] UPPS-P Impulsive Behavior Scale http://www.impulsivity.org/measurement/UPPS_P

[22] Only In Your State https://www.onlyinyourstate.com/florida/best-weather-fl/

[23] Wikipedia, the free encyclopedia https://en.wikipedia.org/wiki/Florida_Today

[24] The days of the press plate are nearly gone https://www.heraldextra.com/news/opinion/herald-editorials/the-days-of-the-press-plate-are-nearly-gone/article_e9cb25c5-1b88-5cdb-8064-14a1cec5c8f7.html

[25] Wikipedia, the free encyclopedia https://en.wikipedia.org/wiki/Antisocial_personality_disorder

[26] Not Just Cubans: Many Latinos Now Call Miami Home https://www.nbcnews.com/news/latino/not-just-cubans-many-latinos-now-call-miami-home-n37241

[27] Cyclothymia Disorder https://www.mayoclinic.org/diseases-conditions/cyclothymia/symptoms-causes/syc-20371275

[28] The Most Deadly Insects in The World https://www.complex.com/pop-culture/2013/10/most-deadly-insects-in-the-world/

[29] Halfway House Origins https://psychology.jrank.org/pages/288/Halfway-House.html#:~:text=In%20late%2018th%2Dcentury%20England,privately%20owned%20U.S.%20halfway%20house.

[30] Songfacts https://www.songfacts.com/facts/leadbelly/midnight-special

[31] SEARCH Homeless Services https://www.searchhomeless.org/about/

[32] Inappropriate Affect Symptoms And Signs
https://www.betterhelp.com/advice/personality-disorders/inappropriate-affect-symptoms-and-signs/
[33] https://www.mcleanhospital.org/about
[34] CNY Central, Brett Hall, Thursday, February 8, 2018
https://cnycentral.com/news/tear-it-down-fix-it-up/tear-it-down-or-fix-it-up-gravina-garden-center-to-be-torn-down
[35] Chronicle, by Nadine Brozan, January 7, 1994
https://www.nytimes.com/1994/01/07/style/chronicle-799300.html
[36] Victor Leong's Memorial Fund
https://www.gofundme.com/f/v6xsekys
[37] Houston Shapes Up
https://www.khou.com/article/news/health/mcallen-named-americas-fattest-city-houston-no-longer-in-top-25/285-d0458c43-4787-4755-8363-053a6348491c#:~:text=Houston%20shapes%20up,longer%20in%20the%20top%2025.
[38] Deena Guzder (July 9, 2010). "Nuclear swords to God's plowshares". *The Washington Post*. Archived from the original on August 7, 2012. Retrieved May 16, 2012.
[39] KLTV ABC Channel 7 January 31, 2007
https://www.kltv.com/story/6015820/houston-police-arrest-and-ticket-man-for-protest-signs/
[40] Way Back Sports https://www.kltv.com/2020/04/09/way-back-sports-houston-astrodome-opened-april/
[41] KLTV ABC Channel 7 January 31, 2007
https://www.kltv.com/story/6015820/houston-police-arrest-and-ticket-man-for-protest-signs/
[42] Houston Chronicle, Cindy George, Published 6:30 am CST, Friday, November 17, 2006 https://www.chron.com/news/houston-texas/article/Bush-protester-who-sued-city-settles-1895840.php
[43] DiGeorge syndrome (22q11.2 deletion syndrome)
https://www.mayoclinic.org/diseases-conditions/digeorge-syndrome/symptoms-causes/syc-20353543#:~:text=DiGeorge%20syndrome%2C%20more%20accurately%20known,development%20of%20several%20body%20systems.
[44] Science Daily, January 4, 2019, Imperial College London
https://www.sciencedaily.com/releases/2019/01/190104103950.htm
[45] Youth Hockey Levels, Explained
https://www.purehockey.com/c/youth-hockey-levels-explained

www.ingramcontent.com/pod-product-compliance
Lightning Source LLC
Chambersburg PA
CBHW031622040426
42452CB00007B/627